Dreams and Visions

Muslims' Miraculous Journey to Jesus

RICK KRONK

DESTINY IMAGE™ EUROPE srl
Via Maiella, 1
66020 San Giovanni Teatino (Ch) – Italy

"Changing the world, one book at a time."

This book and all other Destiny Image™ Europe books are available at Christian bookstores and distributors worldwide.

To order products, or for any other correspondence:

DESTINY IMAGE™ EUROPE srl
Via Acquacorrente, 6
65123 - Pescara – Italy
Tel. +39 085 4716623 - Fax: +39 085 9431270
E-mail: info@eurodestinyimage.com
Or reach us on the Internet: www.eurodestinyimage.com

ISBN: 978-88-89127-89-6
For Worldwide Distribution, Printed in the U.S.A.
1 2 3 4 5 6 7 8 / 14 13 12 11 10

Acknowledgments

Some say it takes a village to raise a child. Similarly, I would say that it takes a community to write a book. First I would like to thank my professors from Dallas Theological Seminary, Dr. Mike Pocock and Dr. Ramesh Richard, who were among the first to encourage my initial research of the phenomenon of dreams and visions.

Second, I would like to thank friends and colleagues who over the years were kind enough to let me talk about my passion for dreams and visions, then show an interest in it, and finally, at least for some, take the time to read and comment on the early versions of the manuscript. Kudos to Brett Cushing, Dawn Edwards, Margaret Niznik, Pat Cate, Joan Swanson, Linda Nuss, and Tim Keuning for their efforts in this vein.

Finally, thanks to those who were willing to share their remarkable encounters with Jesus and for whom life continues to bear the indelible marks of the Divine Dream-giver.

Last but not least, I wish to thank my wife and children, who encourage me every step of the way and without whom this journey called life would be ever so lonely.

Contents

Foreword

Christian ministry among Muslims has always been marked by seemingly insurmountable obstacles. First there are the barriers to belief among Muslims themselves, and secondarily, there are barriers in the minds of Christians regarding outreach to Muslim friends. The biological growth of Islam together with immigration from Muslim countries is bringing Christians and Muslims together as never before. And the question is raised, "How will Christians overcome the obstacles to witness and faith among these peoples?"

Acceptance of dreams and visions as a key factor in belief among Muslims has been hard to assimilate into the Western worldview held by many Christians. And yet, the testimonies in this book give clear evidence that dreams and visions have impacted Muslims and led many to faith in Christ. In addition to recounting stirring firsthand stories of conversion, Rick Kronk also provides a brief history of the development of Islam and why dreams have such importance for Muslims. After dealing with the Church's response to Islam throughout the centuries, he discusses the phenomenon and role of dreams and visions in both the Old and New Testaments and establishes criteria for discerning the reliability of dreams as a basis for belief.

Readers of this book will find themselves encouraged by recent development of witness and response to the Gospel among Muslims that Rick Kronk highlights in this book. They will also find their minds opening to what for many will be a fresh reality, that God is using the same gracious dynamics today to get the attention of unbelievers and show Himself to those who desperately need Him.

Michael Pocock, Chairman and Senior Professor
World Missions and Intercultural Studies
Dallas Theological Seminary

A Dream Encounter With Jesus

God is working among Muslims. I've witnessed His work firsthand. I've talked with converts. I have friends who were Muslims but have come to know Jesus as their personal Savior.

Unfortunately, most of the Western Christian world is unaware of this tangible move of God and is filled with anxiety and doubt with regard to reaching Muslims for Christ. Faced with few personal relationships with Muslims and bombarded by accounts of geopolitical turmoil that has Islamic personalities and nations at the center, Christians wonder if God is even able to penetrate the black veil of ritual and religion that traces its origins to the prophet Mohammad.

Although the world of Islam is expanding—numerically as well as politically and ideologically—God is increasingly bringing Muslims from all walks of life to faith in Jesus Christ, and in many cases, He is using dreams and visions to do so. It is vital that Christians understand this phenomenon of how in many instances Muslims' journey to faith in Christ is nurtured by supernatural events and become willing to reach out to Muslims rather than adopt an attitude of defeat or become antagonistic.

This book is built around the experiences of Muslims who meet Jesus through a dream or a vision, and yet, the phenomenon is not limited to an Islamic encounter with Christianity. With the exception of this first story, the names within the other stories have been changed to protect their identity and privacy. The following story is that of a friend of mine, himself a non-Muslim. When he heard me tell the stories of some of the men and women included in the chapters that follow, he could hardly contain his excitement. I didn't understand why until I read with wonder his following letter to me in which he reveals his own dream encounter with Jesus. Brett's experience that is preserved here is not unique but reflects the experience of many modern-day Christians from the West—an experience that can serve as a bridge linking Western and Muslim supernatural encounters with God via dreams and visions.

❧❧❧❧❧

Dear Rick,

As you know, I was raised with a thoroughly Western worldview and educated in a fine secular university in the United States. A dream encounter with Jesus during my college years not only left me with an unforgettable memory but also changed my life forever. Despite the transforming effect this encounter with Jesus had on my life, the nature of the experience was not something I could easily talk about. Who would have believed me? Not only was my experience unique to those who shared my social and intellectual context, but I also had no biblical or theological categories that would help me to understand it. And so the story lay safely hidden away.

Until I read the manuscript of this book.

When I read your careful biblical exegesis for the first time, I was able to frame my experience in appropriate biblical and theological ways. Your cultural analysis gave me new eyes to see God at work despite my cultural blinders. Finally, as I read the stories of the men and women who bravely tell their own miraculous encounters with Jesus, I felt as if they were telling my story as well. And though I've never been a Muslim, reading of their discovery of the same Jesus allowed me to relive that day nearly 20 years ago when Jesus came to me. Their courage to testify has given me courage to do the same.

So, here is my story. I lived a fairly religious—even Christian—life throughout my childhood and teen years. But increasing family conflict and challenges to my Christian faith in the early years of my college experience led me to an eventual rejection of Jesus Christ. I can still remember the questions with which I fought—questions that were more like accusations than anything else. "What good is this Christian life anyway?" and, "What difference do You make in my life, Jesus?" Frustrated at not finding satisfactory answers to my accusatory questions, I finally challenged Jesus to show Himself to me and prove that He made any difference in my life, or anyone else's, for that matter. At that moment, I knew in my heart that I really didn't want to know. I was turning away from Him in order to live my own life my own way.

And so I did. Freed from the obligations and expectations that the Christian life had always imposed on me, for the next several years, I lived a life that was increasingly marked by selfishness, promiscuity, and debauchery. In the short term, I was happy. I was more and more popular. I was more and more "free" from guilt. And I was having a blast. But for some reason, it didn't seem to last.

The first sign that something was wrong was when I realized that I was needing more and more selfishness, promiscuity, and debauchery to find the same level of "happiness." Next, the realization began to sink in that I was being consumed from the inside out. Though I looked great on the outside, my heart was empty, and I felt increasingly guilty.

One day I was sitting with friends in a dormitory activity center that I managed. Several students from the dorm were listening to me read the notes from the ever-popular and often-comedic suggestion box. However, this time the suggestions took the form of questions. As I read from the papers blindly selected from the suggestion box, instead of ideas of how to improve next weekend's party or a request to host a softball tournament, I found myself reading questions about me. "Brett, what's with you lately? You seem really different." "Brett, where have you gone? We want the old Brett back." "Brett, is everything all right? You seem different." My friends sitting with me agreed with those questions that I had become a different person. People were not commenting that I had been living a different lifestyle but that I had become a different person.

Instantly, I remembered my question to Jesus, my prayer to Him, and my declaration of independence from Him. The answer to my question of whether or not Jesus made a difference in my life came in the form of others' questions inside a suggestion box—which had become a conclusion box. As I continued to read, the verdict became clear: I was different when I refused to yield to Christ. Other people did not like me without Christ; and even more, I did not like me without Christ.

I was overcome by guilt because of my hedonistic lifestyle and my outright rejection of Christ. I had pursued this lifestyle to escape the guilt I experienced from other Christians, but I could not escape the guilt in the form of my own denial. In response, I took a nap.

While I napped, I began to dream, and then suddenly that dream was interrupted and I found myself surrounded by bright light and white clouds. Everything seemed so inviting and tranquil. Then I saw beams of light streaming past me from behind. I felt welcoming warmth upon my back from the light. I turned, and to my astonishment, I saw Jesus Christ looking with intense fondness at me. I not only saw Him, but I also felt in the warmth around Him, His deep love for me. Words could not describe this incredible love and fondness that I felt He had for me. It was the most powerful sensation I had ever experienced. It was so powerful that it drained all the energy from my body.

I wanted to run to Him, I was eager to get to Him, but the intensity of His love for me drained me of my energy, and I fell to the ground, still yearning to be with Him. As I lay on the ground, the huge but gentle hands of Christ swept me up and pulled me in to Him. I felt His embrace. I felt His deep love and longing to be with me. I enjoyed it thoroughly and never wanted to leave. The love of Christ is expressed in the crucifixion of Christ, but the love of Christ I now experienced in this dream was all encompassing.

This enthralling embrace seemed to last for a time immeasurable. And as I looked back over His shoulder, there suddenly appeared a television screen. As I continued hugging Christ, I witnessed on the television screen pictures of everything I had been doing wrong. I saw the promiscuity and the partying, and I felt the guilt all over again. But this time I could not deny it, nor did I want to deny it. Instead, I wanted to confess it and withdraw from Christ's love because of it.

In my utter shame, I began to push myself away from Christ's warm embrace. He looked disappointed that I would want to leave, but He knew why. I told Him, "No, I don't deserve this love." He looked as though still disappointed but shook His head as if He knew something that I did not.

He said to me, "No, you don't understand."

I quickly interjected in a demanding tone and said, "No, no, no, now I understand. I never knew You loved me this much, but look," I said as I pointed to the television screen behind Him, "at the things I've done against you!" I demanded that He look. I wanted to confess it all and then leave His presence of my own volition.

Jesus refused to look at the television screen. Instead, He kept His gaze upon me and smiled in a very understanding way. He said to me in such a kind and gentle tone. "Brett, don't you understand? I knew about those things, and that is why I died for you." He then pointed in reference to the television screen, but without looking at it, and continued, "I died for you so that none of those things would ever come between us. I love you so much that those things will never come between us."

Then I understood. This is a God of grace! I threw my arms around Him and hugged Him again, and He smiled and enjoyed it as much as I did, perhaps even more.

I woke up from the dream drenched in tears of joy after experiencing a God of grace. Not long after the dream, I was in church and I heard the pastor read Isaiah 38:17, "Surely it was for my benefit that I suffered such anguish. In Your love You kept me from the pit of destruction; You have put all my sins behind Your back." I had never heard this passage of Scripture before, but I had seen it in my dream, when Jesus would not look behind Himself to see my sin. I couldn't believe my ears—this passage depicted what I had seen in the dream.

I left my life of partying and promiscuity immediately. I devoted myself to the church and to campus ministry. I had no more desire to live as I did because my God loved me so much. Soon after this, I was at home visiting my parents. As I was about to leave, my mom told me that she had something for me. She brought out a picture entitled "Finally Home," which depicts a person in the clouds experiencing the full embrace of Jesus. I began to weep uncontrollably and told my mom about my dream and about our gracious God shown in the picture.

Rick, today I am the senior pastor of a church in Minnesota—a church of very "normal" Christians with a very Western worldview that often gets in the way of our experiencing God. As I read the manuscript, my heart was stirred and my mind was challenged to take a new look at the world through the lens of Scripture. The testimonies that you include and the explanation of history and Scripture confirm that our gracious God is still at work in the world, and that we should expect God to continue to reveal Himself to us. Thank you for collecting these stories, analyzing cultures, summarizing history and explaining the Scriptures so that I could understand what God was saying to me over 20 years ago. May our gracious God continue to reveal Himself in dreams and visions to our Muslim friends and neighbors as well as to the slumbering church of the West. And may we respond to His revelation so He receives all of the glory.

Your brother in Christ,

Brett

ⰔⰔⰔ

The God of creation and of creativity is not bound by culture or tradition. When He speaks, He does so in order to be heard. Whether dreams and visions are part of your world matters little to the One who needs not ask permission to get your attention. Just as my friend, Brett, learned, a divine interruption can come anytime and anywhere. Are you ready to hear what He has to say?

CHAPTER 1

Ahmad's Story: Against all Reason

All changes, even the most longed for, have their melancholy; for what we leave behind us is a part of ourselves; we must die to one life before we can enter another. —Anatole France

In Caesarea there lived a Roman army officer named Cornelius...One afternoon about three o'clock, he had a vision (Acts 10:1,3 NLT).

The late Dietrich Bonhoeffer said, "When Christ calls a man, He bids him come and die." Bonhoeffer of course is speaking penetratingly here of the radical reorientation of life that comes to those who turn to Christ in faith. For many of us in the West, for whom Christian values find parallels in the wider culture, conversion to Christ may result in behavior that meets with little resistance, even if the prevailing laws of the land intend to favor no specific expression of religious faith. For us, Bonhoeffer's call is a call to personal reform; a dying to self, so as to be able, and rightly so, to follow Christ.

For many others who do not live in this cultural bubble in which Christian values are shared, conversion to Christ can have real, physical consequences. In many instances, Bonhoeffer's call is a literal call to surrender relationships, opportunities, or even one's life. Here is a story that confirms this reality. Ahmad is a friend who heard Christ's call repeatedly. As he pondered Christ's invitation to follow Him, he began to understand the implications of such a choice. While agonizing over the reality of what choosing Christ would mean, Jesus showed up.

ৰ্জ্যৰ ৰ্জ্যৰ ৰ্জ্যৰ

"Do you realize what you've done? How could you do this to your family?" The trembling, angry voice of my sister-in-law, Fatima, continued, "How will you tell your mother and your brothers? You know your mother is not strong, and yet you do something like this?"

"Look," I said, "I'm praying that God will help each of you to accept what I have done. I'd like you to tell the rest of the family for me. Would you please?"

Shocked and dismayed, Fatima said she would, and left my room.

And so it began. The thing I had feared the most, that my mother would suffer, was now inevitable; and worse, it would be because of me. And then I heard it, "Ahmad!" It was my mother's hysterical voice. I didn't want to leave my room. I didn't want to face her, but I knew I must.

I found my mother in the living room, shaking and weeping loudly. When she saw me, her broken voice asked, "How could you do that?" Through her tear-filled eyes she added, "You are no longer my son." Then she began yelling at me and hitting her head with her hands before collapsing in uncontrollable weeping.

A few minutes later, my brother, Ali, arrived. Immediately he knew that something was wrong—seriously wrong. My sister-in-law summarized it well, "Ahmad has become a Christian!"

"What?!" my brother yelled at the top of his voice. Grabbing my short collar with both hands, Ali pulled me in and shouted in my face, "Do you know what you are doing?"

"Yes, I do," was all I could manage to say. He began to push me around, the fury and tears beginning to take him over the edge. I landed in a chair in the corner. At one point another brother, Samir, entered and attempted to come to my rescue, only to be swept aside by Ali.

Somehow I got out of the house. I knew I couldn't stay. The tears and grief of my mother broke my heart. It sounded as if I was attending my own funeral. The anger and mounting violence of my brother scared me, even though I knew he never meant to hurt me. As I made my way down the sidewalk to I didn't know where, I heard the voice of Ali calling after me, "As long as you've found your own God, find your own place!"[1]

Now what? My bitterest dream had now come true—I was disowned by my own family.

How had this happened? What in the world had gotten into me that I would do such a thing—leave Islam for Christianity? If I looked at it logically—and I had a hundred, no more like a thousand times since—it didn't add up. Islam had been my religion from birth, or at least as long as I was conscious of it, and it had served my parents and grandparents, and who knows how many generations of parents before them as well.

Yes, we had left our homeland to come to the United States, leaving behind all that had been familiar to us, and that move had been the hardest thing I had ever done. But we had made other friends here. My brothers got jobs. I was able to go to high school. If anything, the move had made our family better, closer, happier. I had simply no good reason to change, much less to do so by bringing such grief on my mother. How did it happen? At first glance, it didn't seem to make sense. But let me tell you the rest of the story.

I was born into an Asian family that had immigrated to Uganda in the 1880s. In response to a British colonial invitation to build railroads and other economic infrastructure, my ancestors joined thousands of others who left their families, friends, and all things familiar, to start a new life in a far-off African "paradise." Over the years, these hard-working immigrants became the middle-class shopkeepers and merchants of the growing, modernizing Ugandan cities.[2]

Like many Asians, my family was Muslim. Due to the large number of Muslims that had settled in the capital city where I grew up, we were able to maintain and nurture our Islamic faith in the midst of an otherwise foreign culture.

My uncle had at one time predicted that I would grow up to become an Imam—a Muslim cleric. Spurred by this "prophetic" word, I nurtured a hunger to learn the Qur'an and sought to lead a life of Muslim piety from my earliest childhood. As an example of how my faith was taking root, as early as age 5, I joined my parents and older siblings in fasting during the month of Ramadan and began facing Mecca to pray five times a day in keeping with Muslim tradition; something that most boys didn't do until much older.

At age 10, I entered a Quranic contest designed to highlight and reward those who had memorized and could recite the most Quranic passages with the greatest accuracy. Despite my youth as compared to the other contestants, I finished third. Two years later I went to see an Imam to inquire about becoming a student of Urdu, the mother-tongue of my parents. So impressed was the Imam with my mastery of the Quranic Arabic that he agreed to become my teacher and asked me to be an assistant in his Quranic class. With my life's goal of becoming an Imam now on track, I reveled in my place in life.

In January 1971, things changed dramatically for Uganda and subsequently for my family. A military coup d'etat, led by Idi Amin, overturned the British-backed government of Milton Obote. Amin, because of his Muslim faith, was initially seen as a liberator who brought great hope to the Muslims of Uganda. Soon after his takeover of the government, Amin declared himself President for Life and set out to impose a series of reforms designed to remake the country. President-for-Life Amin hunted down any and all sympathizers of the former president. He increased spending on the police and military at the expense of other domestic needs, which brought added hardship to an already-stressed economy. He expelled foreigners, cut off diplomatic relations with Western nations with whom he disagreed, and aligned himself with rogue dictators such as Moammar Qadafi of Libya.

Despite these drastic changes and the resultant, sometimes violent, interventions of police or military in the lives of many of the "normal" citizens of Uganda, my family and I felt reassured that our Muslim faith garnered us good favor in the eyes of Amin's new administration. President Amin was, after all, a Muslim, just like us. However in 1972, within a year of taking power, Amin announced that he had received a message from Allah that he should "Africanize" Uganda and make it the first genuinely black

African state. According to Amin, this meant that all non-Ugandans would have to leave the country—even those who could trace their Ugandan roots back to the 1800s—even those who had never lived outside of Uganda—even me and my family.

Reluctantly and with heavy hearts, we prepared to leave the country that we had grown to love. With the help of the Lutheran Immigration and Refugee Services of the Lutheran Council in America, we were eventually granted refugee status and brought to the United States. After our initial stay in New York City in November 1972, we were taken to Minneapolis, Minnesota, where we were settled in a home in the southern part of the city.

Immediately following my arrival in Minneapolis, I began attending a local vocational high school and I set out to fulfill a dream to become an electrician like my father. Taking an opportunity on Human Relations Day later that year to explain my Islamic faith, I was summarily invited by one student in the audience to attend a Bible study and prayer group that met on Tuesdays before school.

I accepted the invitation to attend the Bible study and prayer meeting so that I could learn more about Christianity. I had no real interest or motivation to embrace the faith of the Christians; rather, I wanted to see these Christians become Muslims. For that to happen, I knew that I would have to have a good understanding of their faith if I was to persuade them that it was wrong. How could I tell them that I was right if I didn't know what they believed?[3]

By attending the Tuesday morning Bible study, I gained little in terms of understanding the Christian faith, but I was increasingly impressed by their lives. They had warmth and compassion. They expressed understanding and love, not only for one another, but also for me. Their conduct and character stood out against that of the rest of the high school students.[4] Furthermore, I was inclined to hang out with these kids because they were among the few students that didn't drink or use drugs—things completely prohibited by Islam. Over the course of the year, I attended as many Tuesday Bible studies and other "Christian" activities as I could. On one occasion I even attended a Youth-for-Christ winter retreat. I went on the retreat, not so much because I wanted to spend that much more time with Christians, but because some of these kids had genuinely become my friends.

Later that year, in response partially to the evangelistic efforts of my classmates, my family and I started a Shiite mosque in the basement of our home. Once all was up and "running," I began to invite kids to meet and share a meal with my family—a chance for them to experience the warmth and hospitality of Islam. I was proud of the fact that my family exhibited joy and unity and had a deep love for each other that my Christian friends felt and admired. The warmth and devotion of my family to one another and to Islam was so powerful that some of the Christian kids began to investigate the teachings and practices of Islam for themselves.

Despite my growing friendship with Christians, one thing that grew increasingly aggravating were the not-so-sensitive attempts to convert me. On one occasion, a couple of kids read through a "4-Spiritual Laws" booklet[5] with me only to conclude by saying, "If you don't accept Jesus Christ as your Savior, you are going to hell." I heard their words, but I couldn't quite grasp what they meant by "accept Jesus as your Savior." In response, I began to memorize the verses from the "4-Spiritual Laws" booklet in my own time so that I could cite them back to the Christians who were using them to try to convert me!

On another occasion a family of one of the Christian kids from school invited me to their home for dinner. I was always glad to share a meal with a nice family, but as the dinner discussion wore on, it became clear to me that they had arranged all of it in order to try to convince me of their Christian faith. Despite my cultural and religious commitment to honoring hosts and humbly accepting hospitality, I finally stood to my feet and said, "If you are trying to make me into a Christian, you are wasting your time and mine!" and walked out.

Slowly, the resentment that had been growing in me toward some Christians turned into hatred. I hated some of them who seemed to be constantly judging me and my faith. I hated being pushed to "accept Jesus" without anyone ever bothering to explain to me what it meant. And I especially hated the fact that no one had taken the time to find out what I believed. I finally told a group of Christians at school, "How do you know if you are right and I am wrong, if you never take the time to find out what I believe?"

I was convinced that Islam was the true faith, that the Qur'an was the final revelation, and that Allah was the one and only God. I loved Islam and I longed to see my friends embrace it as their faith as well. I bristled at the claim that if I did not accept Jesus Christ that I would go to hell. But I was drawn in some inexplicable way to three of my Christian friends, and to one girl in particular. They were different from all the others. For some reason, despite the fact that these three went to church every Sunday, attended Youth for Christ and Campus Life meetings every week, despite the fact that these kids were involved in more Christian activities than any of the others, for some reason none of these kids ever talked to me about Jesus. None of them ever confronted me with "The 4 Spiritual Laws." None of them ever told me that I would go to hell without "accepting Jesus"… whatever that meant.

One day, I was alone with Karen, one of the three, and I asked her, "Karen, what makes you different from the others?" Not knowing how to answer, she said nothing. I added, "I know that you go to church every week. I know that you attend all these Christian meetings after school. You go on retreats and all the rest, but why don't you ever talk to me about Jesus?" After a moment, Karen replied, "Ahmad, since knowing you, I've had the chance to see what Islam is all about. What you and your family have is beautiful. One thing you need to know is that Jesus loves you just the way you are. And because He does so, I do too. But one thing I have that you don't, I know that I am going to Heaven. I have assurance that Jesus died for me and that my sins are forgiven. In order for you to have this, you need to turn your life over to Jesus by confessing your sins and asking him to take control of your life." And then Karen showed me how I could turn my life over to Jesus in prayer.

With this simple yet profoundly caring response to my question, I found myself suddenly stuck. On the one hand what my friend Karen had said was beautiful; and perhaps something inside me wanted it to be true. But on the other hand, I was a Muslim and I knew that there was only one

God, Allah. I knew that according to Islam, Jesus was only a prophet. And, I knew that according to Islam He didn't die on a cross, and He certainly was not raised from the dead!

As I reflected on these things, a foreboding question slowly took shape in my mind, "If for the Muslims there is one God, and for the Christians there is one God, which one is the True God?" The Christians and the Muslims can't both be right because they believe very different things about God. And yet, they both claim to have the truth! Haunted by the implications of this question, I recoiled and began calling out to God in passionate, yet silent prayer, imploring, begging God—whether the Christian God or the Muslim God—to show Himself and settle the issue once for all. For several hours I sat in agony, my spirit yearning for a divine response.

Then suddenly, in the stillness of the room, a man appeared and said in a resonant, reassuring voice, "Come, I will show you the way." Somehow, without the need for any explanation, I knew this to be the voice of Jesus. His invitation to "come" seemed to penetrate all the way to the core of my being. Somehow, I knew in an instant what I had to do; what I wanted to do. Despite all my arguments for Islam and against the Christian faith, despite my feelings of resentment at how some Christians had treated me, despite the imagined reaction of my family members and other Muslim friends, against all apparent reason and with a trembling voice I looked over to Karen and asked her to pray that prayer with me again.

As I prayed, saying, "Jesus I open the door of my heart to you," I saw the Qur'an, and then all of my family, and my mother as they passed before my eyes. Then I confessed my sins and asked Jesus to come and take control of my life. I closed my prayer "in Jesus' name" and joined my friend Karen who was already overcome with emotion. For the first time in my life I felt free.

So that's how it happened. That's what "got" into me that brought me to the place where I could and did renounce Islam and embrace Christianity. Despite all my reasons against the Christian faith, despite the security of my family and their traditions, something bigger and more powerful and more compelling broke through. First there was the Bible that I read and studied with my Christian friends. I knew it to be a holy book, because

Islam said it was—though Muslims believe it has been changed and is no longer dependable. But when I read the accounts of Jesus' life, when I saw Him heal the sick, when I heard Him talk about love and justice and forgiveness, I was drawn to Him. Then it was the friendship of my Christian friends. Some of them really took time for me, cared about me and my problems. Some really tried to understand what I believed and how my family and I lived. They showed deep respect for who I was and where I had come from. That touched me deeply. Finally, the vision of Jesus was simply overwhelming. Seeing Jesus and hearing His voice is an experience that is really beyond words to describe. When you realize that *the* Jesus is speaking to you, how can you resist? Without having to explain, in His invitation to me to "come," I suddenly understood that what the Bible said about love and forgiveness was for me.

In the years since I began to follow Jesus, God has helped me to rebuild my relationship with my family. It has not always been easy—for them or for me. Little by little we began to talk to each other, and later to spend time together. What was important was for them to see that though I had decided to follow Jesus and become a Christian, I had not abandoned my culture, or my morals. It was also important for them to hear and see that I still loved them—that I wanted them to be in my life, and I wanted to be in their lives. We now come and go freely to each other's homes. My mother adored my wife, and my wife loved my mother. We gather frequently for family meals and attend the important events of each other's children. My brothers and their wives continue in their Islamic faith, and though I believe differently, I no longer feel a sense of judgment or rejection. Though we no longer share a common faith, only God knows what He has prepared for them. Perhaps they will, like me, encounter Jesus in a dream or vision that will somehow sweep away all their objections.

৵৵৵৵৵

At the age of 16, Ahmad, a devout Shiite Muslim, had this vision of Jesus. His response to the invitation to "come" led him to leave Islam for Christianity. Such a change, however, did not come without a price. In the weeks following his vision of Jesus and subsequent conversion, his family discovered his new faith. Considered an infidel and traitor, Ahmad was put out of the house. For the first time in his life he was forced to face the world without the love and support of his family. Ahmad turned to his Christian friends and sought out a church. Though no one could pretend to fill the void of his family, several people stood out as true friends with whose help Ahmad was able to survive the aloneness, grow in his faith, and eventually rebuild a bridge back to his family that he enjoys to this day. Today, over 30 years later, the memory of the pain and joy of that time in Ahmad's life— what he refers to as "bittersweet freedom"—is still vivid.

Ahmad is not the only Muslim to have encountered Jesus in this way. Throughout history, stories of Muslims from every walk of life and virtually every cultural context tell of conversions to Christianity prompted by dream or vision experiences. What happened in that supernatural encounter that enabled Ahmad to choose against the strong religious heritage that he enjoyed with his family? What was it about the vision that made it possible for someone like Ahmad to turn his back on his Islamic faith— apparently against all reason?

Are dreams and visions reliable sources of spiritual information? Should they be listened to and followed even if it means leaving one's faith and results in conflict and splitting of families? Should dreams and visions be considered a normal means of conversion for Muslims? What does the Bible have to say about them? Does Church history give us any indication as to how the Church dealt with this phenomenon in the past?

Before we can answer these and other questions that will arise, we need to take a look at the factors that determine the context of our investigation of the phenomenon of dreams and visions. The chapters that follow on the history of Islam and the response of the Christian faith, together with a look at worldviews and the biblical data, are not intended to be exhaustive, but an attempt to bring together the pieces that will help us understand how God is using these supernatural experiences to radically change lives.

Points to Ponder

1. What elements (life experiences, previous knowledge, encounters/discussions with others, etc.) contributed to Ahmad's receptivity to the Gospel message?

2. How does the testimony and influence of Karen differ from other Christians that Ahmad met in high school? What is exemplary in her behavior and words with Ahmad?

3. What does the vision do that Bible studies and discussions with Christians did not? In other words, why was the vision so convincing?

4. How do you account for the response of his family members? What is at stake for them as a result of Ahmad's change of religion?

5. What did Ahmad need most after he announced his faith change to his family? How should the Church provide assistance in cases like this?

CHAPTER 2

The Rise of Islam

A Brief History of Islam—and Modern Anxiety

The whole of history of civilization is strewn with creeds and institutions which were invaluable at first, and deadly, afterwards. —Walter Bagehot

But we preach Christ crucified, to Jews a stumbling block and to Gentiles foolishness. —Apostle Paul, 1 Corinthians 1:23

Islam, which means submission, is the newest of the world's very large religions—those with over 300 million members—that include Christianity, Islam, Hinduism, and Buddhism. Islam's origins can be traced back to the teachings and practices of its founder Mohammad, considered to be the final prophet. He lived in modern-day Saudi Arabia from A.D. 570 to 632. The text that serves as the scriptures for Islam, the Qur'an, was revealed to Mohammad, according to Islamic tradition, in a series of visions spanning some 22 years, in which the angel Gabriel confirmed him as a prophet of God and instructed him to "recite."

It must be remembered that Mohammad did not set out to start a new religion. He saw himself rather as an agent of God who desired to turn his people back to the faith of former prophets, such as Abraham and David. Islamic scholar John Esposito says:

Like his prophetic predecessors, he (the Prophet Mohammad) came as a religious reformer. (He) maintained that he did not bring a new message from a new God but called people back to the one, true God and to a way of life that most of his contemporaries had forgotten or deviated from. Worship of Allah was not the evolutionary emergence of monotheism from polytheism but a return to a forgotten past, to the faith of the first monotheist, Abraham.[1]

As a result of this conviction, Mohammad's teaching initially focused on reform of the idolatrous faith and undisciplined way of life of the Arabic tribes that peopled the area.[2] As part of his reforms, he sought to restore religious faith in one God, Allah.

After ten years of contested preaching resulting in only a handful of followers and plagued by mounting doubts of his own capacity to bring about lasting change, Mohammad immigrated to the city of Medina in A.D. 622. Over the next ten years and until his death in A.D. 632, Mohammad's religious, political, and military efforts to reform the spiritual climate of the Arab peninsula led him to become the most powerful leader in Arabia. In turn, Islam became the defining faith that reunited the Arabic peoples. (Refer to Table 1 for a summary of the basic tenets of Islam.)

Fueled by its eventual success in the Arab peninsula, Islam was not content to sit idly by. By 750, Islam had invaded China and India and had begun to make its move along the Mediterranean coast of North Africa and into Europe. Aided by religious fervor of the growing Muslim community and the inability of opposing nations to respond theologically, militarily, or politically, Islam advanced rapidly. Despite their defeat at the battle of Tours, France, by Charles Martel,[3] Muslim invaders were able to seize and eventually control the territory of modern-day Spain, which they held at least in part until the 15th century.

Doctrine[4]	Practice[5]—The Five Pillars + 1
God: supreme, eternal deity of creation who stands uniquely in undivided oneness. Considered all powerful, merciful, wise, all-knowing, and far above human description and comprehension.	**Prayer (salat):** Ritualized prayer in which the orientation (facing Mecca), form/style and words are prescribed at five specific times of the day (Surah 1:1-7).

Doctrine[4]	Practice[5]—The Five Pillars + 1
Scripture: The message sent from Allah to call people to repentance and renew their faith. The Qur'an being the final message (revelation) from Allah, confirms earlier Scripture and perfects the truth.	**Confession of faith (shahada):** The basic statement of faith which defines Islamic faith and commitment, "There is no God but Allah, and Mohammad is his messenger" (Surah 4:48).
God: supreme, eternal deity of creation who stands uniquely in undivided oneness. Considered all powerful, merciful, wise, all-knowing, and far above human description and comprehension.	**Prayer (salat):** Ritualized prayer in which the orientation (facing Mecca), form/style and words are prescribed at five specific times of the day (Surah 1:1-7).
Scripture: The message sent from Allah to call people to repentance and renew their faith. The Qur'an being the final message (revelation) from Allah, confirms earlier Scripture and perfects the truth.	**Confession of faith (shahada):** The basic statement of faith which defines Islamic faith and commitment, "There is no God but Allah, and Mohammad is his messenger" (Surah 4:48).
Prophets/Apostles: Those upon whom Allah has bestowed the office of prophet or apostle to proclaim the news of Allah (as a prophet) or carry his message (revelation) (as an apostle). Mohammad being the last of the prophets/apostles is the most revered.	**Almsgiving (zakat):** Obliged contribution amounting to 2½ percent of accumulated wealth and assets to be given to the mosque for distribution to the poor and needy (Surah 2:261,262,264,265).
Angels/Demons: Immortal creatures serving as messengers, guardians or recorders (of men's deeds). Demons followed satan in rebellion and now seek to tempt men to evil.	**Fasting during Ramadan (sawm):** Month-long fast from sunrise to sundown during which the faithful refrain from food and drink, tobacco, and sexual relations (Surah 2:183).
Predestination: The supreme sovereignty of Allah results in a final understanding that all is predetermined (mektub—literally, "it is written").	**Pilgrimage to Mecca (Hajj):** Prescribed visit to holiest sites in Islam for the purpose of cleansing the soul (Surah 2:196-207).

Doctrine[4]	Practice[5]—The Five Pillars + 1
Judgment/Last Day: Moment of final reckoning in which Allah distinguishes those worthy of paradise from those deserving hell based upon accumulated good works.	**Struggle (jihad):** The effort, both individual and communal, to fight for the faith and against unbelief. Most understand this as personal struggle against temptation though some take this to mean armed struggle against unbelievers (Surah 2:190-193).

Islam continued to spread and consolidate its power under various rulers (caliphs) throughout the 9th and 10th centuries. In 1095, at the urging of Pope Urban II and for the next 250 years, waves of "Crusaders" fought to liberate formerly Christian lands, and in particular, the city of Jerusalem, from Muslim domination. Despite the exchange of culture and the accelerated opening of trade routes that stimulated some of the European economies, the Crusades, with regard to inter-religious dialogue and cross-cultural relationship, were a colossal failure. Thousands of combatants died—many en route to the place of confrontation. Thousands more citizens of Muslim-controlled territories were killed, regardless of their religious identity. In the end, what the Western Crusaders had gained by military conquest was summarily lost through subsequent political failure to manage and defend it. Furthermore, the Crusades sowed seeds of resentment between Islam and Christianity that have festered for the past 1,000 years.

Following the Crusades, the Muslim world was battered by invasions and quests for control from other rising powers including the Mongols, the Mamluke Turks, and the Persians. In the late 13th century, the Ottoman Turks began to assert their presence and authority in the Muslim world eventually uniting the various factions under the Ottoman Empire. At its zenith, under the reign of Sultan Süleyman the Magnificent in the 16th century, the empire stretched from Algeria in the west to beyond Baghdad in the east, from Egypt in the south to modern-day Hungary in the north.

The Ottomans effectively controlled the Muslim world and the Mediterranean basin for nearly 600 years, though weakened over time by internal power struggles and external conflicts. However, by the late 1800s not much remained of the once mighty empire. Further rebellion and power struggles in the early 20th century eventually led to the dissolution of the Ottoman Caliphate in 1922 by Kemal Ataturk, who launched subsequent reforms that brought about the modernization of Turkey.[6] Despite the demise of the Ottoman Empire, which was to be the last Muslim empire, Islamic identity was still alive and well. The removal of a unified political and religious structure gave Islam a new opportunity to express itself in individual nation-states (such as Syria, Lebanon, Iraq, and Jordan), which were established as a result of the partitioning of the empire by the British and the French following World War I.

The years that followed World War I saw the rise of Arab nationalism, the emergence of oil-wealth, especially in Saudi Arabia, and later the partitioning of the Indian subcontinent into India (a Hindu state) and Pakistan (a Muslim state) in 1947. Additional political dealings together with military and political skirmishes between Western powers and Arab states resulted in the establishment of a Jewish homeland in part of Muslim Palestine in 1948. Subsequent Jewish immigration to the newly founded Israeli state together with unfavorable political, economic, and military exchanges between the Palestinians and the Israelis have resulted in on-again, off-again conflict that continues today.

And yet, despite a history marked by conflict, which at times involved various Western powers, the Muslim world, by and large, had little impact on the life of the average person in the West. In fact, apart from foreign documentaries that highlighted glories of long-lost eras and occasional nightly news reports from some far-off conflict, much of the West remained functionally ignorant of Islam and its followers until the latter-quarter of the 20th century.

But all that was destined to change. Eventually, Muslim identity found the tools it needed to impose itself onto the global agenda. Feeling that they were no longer obliged to remain under the thumb of Western powers, Muslims "awoke" and asserted their independence. Several incidents from 1970 to 1990 serve to highlight the impact of a revived Islam that has thrust itself onto the world stage.

On October 15, 1973, the Organization of Arab Petroleum Exporting Countries (OAPEC) announced an oil embargo against the U.S. in response to the U.S. decision to resupply the Israeli army during the Yom Kippur War. Six months later, OAPEC lifted the embargo after an Israeli troop withdrawal and promise of a negotiated peace between Israel and Syria.[7] Eventually, Israel and its Western allies were able to arrive at a settlement but not before the Muslim world demonstrated its ability to forever influence global economic and political affairs.

Before the decade had passed, another incident pushed the Muslim world into the foreground of global concern. After decades of tension fueled in part by efforts to modernize and secularize the country, Mohammad Reza Pahlevi, the Shah of Iran, was deposed in January 1979. His flight to Egypt, where he later died, opened the door for the return of Ayatollah Ruallah Khomeini from exile. Shortly after his return, the Ayatollah was named supreme ruler and established an Islamic Republic that increasingly embraced fundamentalist Islamic culture and rhetoric, complicating Western nations' relationships with Iran to this day.

On August 2, 1990, Iraq President Saddam Hussein, in an effort to gain additional oil reserves and subsequent influence in the Middle East, invaded Kuwait. The response from a coalition of largely Western countries resulted in the first Gulf War that turned back the Iraqis and restored captured territory to the Kuwaitis. The conflict, tagged by Saddam as "the Mother of all wars," resulted in considerable disappointment across the Islamic world due to the rapid and humiliating defeat of the Iraqis at the hands of "infidels."

In September 2001, hijacked U.S. commercial airplanes were flown into the twin towers of the World Trade Center in New York City and the Pentagon in Washington DC. These attacks claimed the lives of more than 2,700 and injured more than 6,000 people from over 90 different nations. The response from the U.S. led to a coalition-based effort to overthrow Iraq's President Saddam Hussein, a suspected accomplice and supposed detainee of a cache of weapons of mass destruction, and hunt down and try Osama bin Laden, the outspoken *provocateur* and mastermind of the 9/11 attacks. The ensuing Iraq war and the related conflict with bin Laden sympathizers, the Taliban in Afghanistan, have eroded positive sentiment toward the U.S. across the Muslim world.

These events, together with more recent events such as the March 2004 train bombings in Madrid, the killing of Dutch filmmaker Theo Van Gogh in November 2004, and the July 2005 bombings of the London transport system, have served to put Muslims and the religion of Islam on the front page of newspapers worldwide.

In addition to bringing Islam into everyday conversation not just of politicians and newscasters, but of school teachers and business leaders, these events have also served to raise the level of global anxiety. Muslims, who were consistently portrayed as being out-of-step with the modern West, have in recent years acquired state-of-the-art technological know-how, amassed significant wealth—due largely to oil revenues—and attained considerable international political clout. As a result, they have become worrisome to many. Anti-Western tirades, emotional public protests, and dramatic violence have prompted many Western nations to redesign security agencies and practices in an effort to protect their people, infrastructure, and resources from a perceived global menace that wears an Islamic face.

To add to its geopolitical saber rattling, which has the West scrambling to build protective barriers against destructive Islamic elements, Islam has another trick up its sleeve: religious resurgence. Despite the majority position Christianity retains over the world's religions, the rate of growth of Christianity has been recently superseded by the worldwide growth of Islam. Estimates of religious affiliations had expected an increase in Islam from nearly 20 percent of the world's population in 2000 (approximately 1.2 billion Muslims out of nearly 6 billion total global population) to nearly 25 percent in 2050.

However, a recent report on the size and distribution of the world's Muslim population by the Pew Research Center indicates that Islam has already attained that mark. According to the study released in October 2009, the global Muslim population is estimated to number 1.57 billion, or 23 percent of the world's population estimated to be 6.8 billion.[8]

Islam's rapid growth is primarily the result of higher birthrates, although significant conversion growth has occurred in parts of Africa and

Indonesia.[9] But Islam has not only contented itself with growth in the Far East and Africa. The fallout of nominal Christians from the church in traditionally Christian Western nations over the last century has left a vacuum of religious faith into which Islam and other religious faiths have moved. According to Abdul-Haqq:

> Islam…has already made spiritual gains among the spiritually disaffected…This initial success has imported a euphoria to its missionary strategists so that they are now dreaming of and planning for the Islamization of the Western Hemisphere. The time is not too far away when people on the American and European Continents will be confronted with the challenge of Islam in a way unknown in history.[10]

Chillingly prophetic, these words from nearly 30 years ago have suddenly become a framework within which to try to understand the rise of Islam beyond the borders of traditionally Muslim lands. Though Muslims are still a small minority in the West, constituting only about 5 percent of Europe's total population (approximately 38 million Muslims out of approximately 730 million people[11]), certain demographic trends suggest that significant change is forthcoming.

First, consider the fact that Muslims in general maintain a significantly higher birth rate than many non-Muslims. Second, Muslims from many often-troubled nations are on the move as immigrants for both economic and political reasons. An estimated one million legal and nearly 500,000 illegal immigrants enter Europe each year, many of whom are Muslims from North Africa, Turkey, and other Islamic countries. Third, Muslim immigrants are often highly religious and find themselves immediately in conflict with liberal, and now largely secular, cultures of formerly Christian European nations.

How significant is Muslim immigrant growth in Europe? In an April 10, 2006, speech on Al Jazeera, Libyan President Muammar al-Gaddafi said this, "There are signs that Allah will grant victory to Islam in Europe without swords, without guns, without conquest. We don't need terrorists, we don't need homicide bombers. *The 50-plus million Muslims (in Europe) will turn it into a Muslim continent in a few decades."*

In an effort to respond to the growing size and public presence of Islam in their midst, many European nations in particular are investigating changes to public policy in order to encourage and accelerate the process of integration while at the same time establishing stiffer immigration and anti-terror measures. Consider the following:

1. In July 2004, it was reported that the Spanish government began formal discussions to subsidize mosque construction in an effort to make them less dependent on financing from extremist groups. In an address before the Spanish Parliament, Jesus Nunez Villaverde, director of the Institute for the Study of Conflicts and Humanitarian Action said, "The state must do more to dilute the presence of fundamentalist religious expression that is financed through its own channels, and for which we have not one single instrument of influence, contact or association."[12]

2. In November 2004, Nicolas Sarkozy, the then French Minister of the Interior, went on record affirming that some kind of affirmative action program was necessary to further Muslim integration and suggested that one way to do this was for the state to assist in funding mosque construction in order to help create a French version of Islam. In responding to an interviewer's question about the compatibility of Islam with the republican values of France, Sarkozy replied, "It is too late to raise the compatibility issue. Whether I like it or not, Islam is the second biggest religion in France. So you've got to integrate it by making it French."[13]

As a result of follow-through on Sarkozy's suggestion, an article notes that French public authorities are subsidizing up to 30 percent of mosque construction. The same article quotes former president of the French Council of the Muslim Faith, Dalil Boubaker, saying, "Today, mayors are the foremost constructors of mosques [in France]."[14]

3. In a story published by the British Broadcasting Corporation (BBC) February 7, 2008, Dr. Rowan Williams, the Archbishop of Canterbury, suggested that the British Government would be well-served to adopt some elements of Sharia (Islamic) law in an effort to accommodate its Muslim citizens. In an interview with Radio 4's "World at One," Dr. Williams "argued that adopting parts of Islamic Sharia law would help maintain social cohesion. For example, Muslims could choose to have marital disputes or financial matters dealt with in a Sharia court." Furthermore, he added, "Muslims should not have to choose between 'the stark alternatives of cultural loyalty or state loyalty.'"[15]

Many other incidents could be added to this list, but even these few demonstrate clearly that the presence of Islam has been seriously elevated in the West. Due to a media-fueled anxiety coupled with a general lack of firsthand knowledge of Muslims, the non-Muslim world is left often to conclude that these people want nothing but conflict and will settle for nothing but conquest. And the evidence, unfortunately, supports the conclusion. Speaking of the propensity toward violence in the Muslim world, Samuel Huntington notes that despite the fact that "Muslims make up about one-fifth of the world's population…in the 1990s they have been far more involved in intergroup violence than the people of any other civilization. The evidence is overwhelming."[16]

Even the global Christian Church is full of anxiety and doubt with regard to the position it should take in response to Islam. Although the biblical mandate to love one's enemies is well known and easily cited, the question of how to respond to a subway bombing or televised hate speech directed at the so-called "Christian West" is not so easily answered. Following the first Gulf War and even more so following the 9/11 attacks, publishers in the West were inundated with books about Islam and the Church's response to it. And yet the underlying sentiment remained that of a palpable uneasiness on the one hand, and a striving to know how to reach these people for Christ before being overrun by them, on the other.

Faced with few personal relationships with Muslims and bombarded by accounts of geopolitical turmoil that has Islamic personalities and nations at the center, many Christians wonder if God is even able to penetrate the black veil of ritual and religion whose followers adhere to a worldview of vastly different beliefs and values,[17] have amassed considerable wealth with which they are able to funds their expansionist agenda,[18] and are increasingly present in sufficient numbers so as to influence local public policy.[19]

The questions raised by this recent Islamic surge are many and range from the political to the cultural and religious. But one question resides behind them all and asks, "Is Islam destined to fulfill its ambition?" Or, asked differently, "Is the current growth of Islam destined to remain unchecked?" From the perspective of the Church the question looks like this, "Does the Gospel—the message of the Church—have anything to say to Islam?"

⌖⌖⌖⌖⌖

Points to Ponder

1. Describe the origins of Islam. Who was involved and where did it all begin?

2. What factors have contributed to the growth of Islam from a local and later regional religion to a global force today?

3. How have recent events in the last half of the 20th century and first few years of the 21st century influenced the way Islam is perceived by the West? How do you think the West is perceived by Muslims living outside the West?

4. What have Western governments done to respond to the growth of Muslim immigration? How does what they have done reflect how they feel about Muslim immigration?

5. To what extent do you think an on-going conflict between Muslim and Western civilizations is inevitable? What should Muslim and Western leaders do to minimize such conflict?

CHAPTER 3

The Gospel and Islam—the Phenomenon of Dreams and Visions

Preach the Gospel at all times and when necessary, use words.
—Saint Francis of Assisi

But you will receive power when the Holy Spirit comes upon you. And you will be My witnesses, telling people about Me everywhere—in Jerusalem, throughout Judea, in Samaria, and to the ends of the earth. —Jesus, Acts 1:8 NLT

Though the first couple of centuries of Islamic history brought Christians and Muslims into contact with one another—though often in conflict due to the expansionist designs of Islam in many cases—missionary efforts directed toward Muslims were overshadowed by other interests and concerns, both from within and without the Church.

In 1095, Pope Urban II called for the establishment of an army to come to the aid of the Church in the east that had been repeatedly attacked and defeated by the Turks and the Arabs. As mentioned previously, for the next 200 years a series of nine Crusades[1] enlisted the aid of Christians from Western Europe in an effort to take back lands (and Jerusalem in particular) that had been won and were being ruled by Arab and Turkish Muslims. Though the details of the Crusades and their effects on culture and commerce of the Medieval Period have been the subject of numerous works, in terms of Christo-Islamic relations, the Crusades fueled resentment, bitterness, and animosity among the Christians and Muslims who survived, hindering mission efforts into the modern era.

However, not all professing Christians of this period were convinced that violence was the only way to engage the Muslim population. In the early 12th century, Peter the Venerable, Abbott of the Benedictine monastery in Cluny located in the Burgundy region of France, became convinced that a different approach to Islam was necessary, one which involved the study of Islam from its own sources. To do so, however, required significant effort to translate pertinent Arab works into Latin, which was carried out by groups of Arabic-speaking Christian scholars who lived and worked in Spain and Sicily, locations that had both been returned from Islamic to Christian rule.

In response to some of these works, Peter the Venerable responded by writing two volumes of his own. The first, *The Entire Heresy of the Saracens*, was, as the title suggests, a summary of Islamic doctrine. His second book, *The Refutation of the Sect or Heresy of the Saracens*, was designed to provide a Christian response to Islam, which, in keeping with other of his contemporaries, he considered to be a form of Christian heresy rather than a separate religion. In taking up the pen, instead of the sword (in stark contrast to the Crusaders of his era—and in opposition to the opinion of his friend, Bernard of Clairvaux), Peter was intent on informing and correcting the followers of Islam. His message was not just educational but overtly evangelical as well, and included an explicit invitation to experience Christian salvation.[2]

The efforts of Peter the Venerable to engage Muslims intellectually and spiritually instead of militarily paved the way for others who continued in this vein. Of note, Roger Bacon, in his treatise composed for Pope Clement IV between 1266 and 1268, argued that "Christianity had been misguided in its aims, which were more concerned with domination than with conversion, and had relied on inadequate methods; preaching, he suggested, was the only way to realize the expansion of Christendom in the future, and to that end languages had to be learnt, other beliefs had to be studied, and arguments had to be formulated in order to refute them."[3]

Translation of Arabic works continued in Spain and to a lesser extent in Sicily throughout the 12th and 13th centuries. As a result of this great influx of material on logic, philosophy, mathematics, physics, medicine, geography, and politics, late medieval Europe found itself being shaped intellectually and culturally by Islam.[4] And from this firsthand look into Arab and Islamic culture, a more realistic picture of Islam began to emerge, an Islam that was able to contribute to the reawakening and civilizing of Europe.

Despite the fact that a certain contingent of Europe continued to pursue a crusading agenda as a means to encounter (and conquer!) Islam, others continued in the spirit of Peter the Venerable. One of the most notable from this era is Saint Francis of Assisi (1181-1226). Saint Francis promoted love instead of hate as the way to win Muslims. Though his early missionary efforts were unsuccessful, he eventually gained an audience with the Sultan of Egypt in 1219. Despite language barriers that hindered a deep and thorough exchange of ideas, Saint Francis was able to communicate the gospel in simple terms. Although the evidence of fruit of his efforts among the Muslims is scant, his example encouraged others to pursue compassion rather than conquering as a motivation for encounter.[5]

Following in the footsteps of Saint Francis, Raymond Lull was the next Christian missionary to leave his mark on missionary efforts to Muslims. Born into a wealthy Catholic family in Majorca, Spain, in 1232, Lull's adolescence and early adult years were marked by immorality and debauchery. In his thirties he had a visionary encounter with Jesus, "hanging on the Cross, the blood trickling from His hands and feet and brow, (who was) look(ing) reproachfully at him." Lull tried to ignore the vision, returning to his immoral pastimes, but the vision returned the following week. This time he surrendered to the Jesus on the Cross and, in keeping with the response to the call to Christian service that was in vogue in his day, Lull embraced a monastic way of life marked by fasting, prayer, and meditation. A second vision some time later prompted Lull to direct his life to missions and in particular, to taking the Christian faith to the Muslims.[6]

Lull spent the next several years in preparation, learning Arabic and disposing of his earthly riches. Finally, after the age of 40, Lull embarked on his missionary career that was driven by three passions: apologetics, education, and evangelism. With regard to apologetics, in addition to the approximately 60 books he wrote on various aspects of the defense of the Christian faith, Lull developed a system designed to persuade non-Christians, and Muslims in particular, of the truth of Christianity. As an example of his strategy, when at last he arrived in Tunis, the capitol of Tunisia, Lull called a conference with local Muslim leaders to "debate the relative merits of Christianity and Islam, promising that if Islam was demonstrated to be superior, he would embrace it as his faith."[7]

In the realm of education, Lull advocated for the creation of training centers throughout Europe which, built on a monastic model, would serve to train Christian ministers for missionary ministry to Muslims. In addition, he lobbied for and finally won the right to have the Arabic language taught in European universities, a step, Lull hoped, would enable dialogue between Christians and Muslims.

But Lull was not content simply to labor to change the attitude of the Church with regard to Muslims; he was also driven to preach the gospel. Over the course of his 40-plus years of missionary activity, and right up until his martyrdom in Algeria in 1315, Lull traveled repeatedly into North Africa for the express purpose of preaching and defending the Christian faith. One biographer summarized the final era of his life like this:

> Lull was influenced by the spirit of the times in which he lived, and "among the Franciscan order, a mania for martyrdom prevailed." To die in the service of his Master would be the highest privilege. So in 1314 he returned to Bugia (Algeria) to see his little band of converts and to put his defense of Christianity to the final test. "For over ten months the aged missionary dwelt in hiding, talking and praying with his converts and trying to influence those who were not yet persuaded...at length, weary of seclusion, and longing for martyrdom, he came forth into the open market and presented himself to the people as the same man whom they had once expelled from their town. ...He pleaded with love, but spoke plainly the whole truth. ... Filled with fanatic fury at his boldness, and unable to reply

to his arguments, the populace seized him, and dragged him out of the town; there by the command, or at the connivance of the king, he was stoned to death on the 30th of June, 1315."[8]

The centuries that followed the death of Lull were all but void of new missionary efforts directed toward the Muslims as the Church, awed in part by the challenge of reaching the Muslim population, became preoccupied with work in more responsive areas of the world. However, the founding of the Jesuits by Ignatius Loyola in the 16th century propelled Catholic missions to the forefront. Soon after, men like Jerome Xavier (1549-1617) found themselves at the center of Christian-Muslim encounter.[9]

In 1579, Xavier along with two other Jesuit comrades traveled to India at the invitation of the Mughal emperor, Akbar, for whom religion held both a personal and political interest. Following discussions and debates with the emperor and Muslim scholars of the empire, Akbar engaged the Jesuits in the education of his son, Murad, with the intent that he would learn the Portuguese language and the Christian faith. Despite the progress made by Murad under his Jesuit tutors, the Christian doctrines of the sonship of Jesus and the Trinity stood in the way of the emperor's willingness to embrace the Christian faith, and Xavier and company returned empty-handed to Portugal in 1583, only four years after their arrival.[10]

Nearly ten years later, in 1593, a second mission was sent to Emperor Akbar. Xavier, again the leader of the expedition, had made a great effort since his last visit to learn Persian and have numerous Christian documents translated into the Persian language. Again, the emperor remained unconvinced and prior to his death he established his own monotheistic faith, which borrowed elements from both Islam and Christianity. Following Akbar's death, the Jesuits entertained hopes that his successor, Jahangir, might be more responsive to their message. In 1610, Jahangir ordered that three of his nephews were to be instructed in the Christian faith and baptized. But within two years, the three recanted, returning to their former belief systems, and the Jesuits returned once again to Europe with no evidence of lasting fruit.[11]

The Reformation that swept across Europe in the 16th century, which began as an effort to reform the Roman Church but resulted in the establishment of Protestantism, opened new doors to mission with a renewed emphasis on the Bible as the source of authority. However, a self-limiting theology of missions[12] together with religious-political conflicts—violent in many cases—resulting from the Protestant hemorrhage, stalled Protestant missions until the emergence of the Pietest movement in the 18th century with its emphases on the invisible church (as opposed to the state-church) and the necessity of personal salvation as the mark of true faith.[13] And yet, it was not until the late 19th century, spurred by the Student Volunteer Movement,[14] that the next notable Christian missionary to Muslims, Samuel Zwemer, emerged.

Samuel Zwemer was born in 1867 into a Christian family in Holland, Michigan, for which Christian service was the norm. Though Zwemer's father was a Reformed Church pastor and four of his brothers entered church ministry, Zwemer felt compelled to follow his sister (who eventually spent 40 years as a missionary in China) into missionary service. Following seminary studies and medical training, Zwemer and fellow seminarian, James Cantine, applied for missionary service to, and were subsequently refused by, the Reformed (mission) Board to prepare for service among Muslims.[15] In response, Zwemer and his friend organized their own agency: the American Arabian Mission. After months of support-raising, Cantine and Zwemer eventually arrived in the Persian Gulf in 1889 and 1890, respectively. Following five years of slow progress, Zwemer married a missionary nurse from England and after a furlough in 1897, returned with his wife to Bahrain.

In addition to local evangelistic activity that he shared with his wife, Zwemer was increasingly sought after to fill promotional and administrative roles in the growing missionary community. In 1906, Zwemer was asked to serve as chairman of the first general missionary conference on Islam that was held in Cairo, Egypt.[16] Later, while in the U.S. speaking about missions and raising funds, he was asked to assume the role of traveling secretary for the Student Volunteer Movement. It was not until after the Edinburgh Missionary Conference of 1910 that Zwemer and his wife were able to return to evangelistic mission activity in the Middle East.

Though living conditions and schooling needs prompted the return of Zwemer's wife and children to the U.S., Zwemer labored on solo. In 1912, the United Presbyterian Mission called him to Cairo, Egypt, to "coordinate the missionary work to entire Islamic world."[17] Zwemer continued his work in Cairo until 1929, at which time he returned to the U.S. to become the chairman of History and Religion and Christian Missions at Princeton.

Zwemer's life was full. In addition to his pioneer evangelistic efforts in the Persian Gulf and the administrative roles he held in mobilizing and training for missions, Zwemer crisscrossed the globe for speaking engagements, for 40 years he edited the *Moslem World* missionary journal, he authored hundreds of missionary tracts and nearly 50 books.[18]

As the Student Volunteer Movement pushed missions forward with literally thousands of eager recruits, denominational missions (like the Reformed Board) were influenced to consider directing some of their energies and resources to reaching Muslims. Though the Anglican Church was among the first to send missionaries to Muslim lands as early as the 1860s, it wasn't until later that the Presbyterians, Methodists, Baptists, and the Christian and Missionary Alliance, together with a number of "faith" missions, joined them.

But the interest in mission's activity directed toward Muslims was not limited to the general rise in mission's activity at the turn of the 20th century. Rather, with the increase in Muslim awareness across the globe—especially in the second half of the 20th century—combined with a heightened evangelical focus and emphasis on the status of the unreached[19] (of which Muslims make up a large percentage) through conferences (such as the triennial Urbana Missions Conference), publications (such as the *World Christian Encyclopedia* first published in 1982), and organizations whose aim is to educate the church about Islam (such as the Zwemer Institute),[20] the number of missions and missionaries who are directly involved in gospel work among Muslims continues to grow.

In light of the tremendous amount of attention given to missionary efforts among Muslims together with the emergence and establishment of Muslim-convert churches across the Muslim world, the question of assessment must be raised. Among those questions that the Church is compelled to ask are the following:

+ What evidence is available to demonstrate that missionary efforts are or have been effective in bringing the gospel to these people?

+ How many Muslim converts from Islam to Christianity are there?

+ What methods, strategies, or tools contribute the most from a human point of view to a clear proclamation and defense of the gospel?

+ What is the status of the relationship between the pioneer missionary, the established missionary, and the Muslim-convert church?

Clearly, answers to these questions (and others like them) are not easy to find, in part because such answers inevitably vary from country to country and are constantly in flux due to social, political, and spiritual factors outside of the control of any agency or church. And yet, as long as there are men and women in need of the gospel, the Church's missionary task requires the pursuit of appropriate means and methods to demonstrate and articulate the gospel among our Muslim neighbors, whether they are local or global.

Despite the political, cultural, and religious challenges that Islam poses to much of the world, reports from many countries, even Islamic ones, give evidence that Muslims are responding to the Christian message of peace, hope, and love. Though numbers are hard to verify, clearly something is stirring in the Muslim world. From the conversion of numerous Javanese Muslims in the 1960s[21] to the sweeping movement of God among the Kabyle Berbers of Algeria in the late 1990s and early 2000s,[22] the reality of Muslim conversion to Christianity—and in many instances in large numbers—is no longer relegated to missiological speculation.

And Christians are not the only ones talking about it. A wide-spread report of a December 2001 al Jazeera interview with Saudi cleric Sheikh Ahmad al Qataani, reveals that Muslim conversion to Christianity can no longer be denied or ignored by Muslims. In the interview, al Qataani comments that indeed the rate of conversion from Islam to Christianity is alarming and he goes on to say that, "Every day, 16,000 Muslims convert to Christianity. Every year, 6 million Muslims convert to Christianity."[23] Though he does not offer the sources for his data nor explain why so many Muslims are converting to Christianity, his admission of the reality of Muslim conversion is enough to establish the fact that it is happening and can no longer be dismissed.

Fuller Evangelical Seminary Professor J. Dudley Woodbury describes the results of a survey he conducted with nearly 750 converts from a Muslim background. The survey was designed in an effort to determine the elements that helped Muslim men and women understand the Christian gospel and put their trust in Christ, resulting in a conversion from Islam to Christianity. Those who participated in the survey represented some 30 countries, 50 ethnic groups, and virtually every major region of the Muslim world. From the compiled results, Woodbury was able to identify several major categories of influences that helped bring a Muslim from Islam to Christianity.

First in the order of significance was seeing the Christian faith lived out. The power of God's love, compassion, and forgiveness demonstrated on a firsthand basis was overwhelmingly compelling to many. As noted in an article that appeared in the October 2007 issue of *Christianity Today*, "A North African Sufi mystic noted with approval that there was no gap between the moral profession and the practice of Christianity he saw."[24] Another testimony of "an Egyptian believer contrasted the love of a Christian group at an American University with the unloving treatment of Muslim students and faculty he encountered at a university in Medina."[25] Others were impressed with the quality of Christian marriages. Still others were attracted by the humility and piety of Christian workers who had come to live among them.

Second, Muslims were affected by the power of answered prayers and healing. For many Muslims, nothing is more dramatic than having God intervene in their personal affairs in response to prayer, especially when the God of Islam is considered to be above caring for man's particular needs. For one young Tunisian, seeing God answer "to the penny" her prayer for a long-overdue raise at work was enough to convince her that God was indeed present and interested in her life. Years of intellectual pursuit came to an end as she surrendered herself to the God who answers prayer.

Third, many Muslims were attracted to Christ as a result of hearing or reading the message of the gospel. Though Muslims are taught that the Christian Scriptures have been corrupted, the simple reading or hearing of the biblical account is often enough to lead some to faith. For many, Jesus' Sermon on the Mount depicts justice and compassion in a way they've never before imagined. For others it is simply the accounts of Jesus' life and miracles that confirm for them that He is Someone unique. One West African, as reported by Woodbury, "was surprised by God's love for all people, even enemies."[26]

One surprising element emerged from the survey. According to more than 25 percent of the nearly 750 respondents, that which was most significant in leading them to faith in Jesus Christ was the experience of a dream or a vision. Furthermore, the survey noted that fully 40 percent of all the respondents experienced a dream or vision event at the time of, or as a precursor to, their conversion, and 45 percent experienced a similar event following their conversion that served as a confirming sign from God.[27] A far less systematic assessment but no less dramatic picture of the importance of dreams and visions was acknowledged by a second-generation Christian worker in Turkey who said that *all* of the Turkish Christians that he had met in his growing up years in Turkey had come to faith in Christ as a result of a dream or a vision.[28]

Despite long periods of Church history in which missions efforts toward Muslims were marked by violence or simply neglect, the examples of a few spirit-filled pioneers paved the way for revived evangelistic activity motivated by love and compassion. In the 19th and 20th centuries, as denominations and faith missions invested resources, Muslims embraced the Christian faith, and sometimes in great numbers.

The resurgence of Islam in the past 30 years combined with a revived evangelicalism in missions have raised the question of effectiveness and an attempt to identify the most productive tools, methods, and strategies. In the midst the necessary yet complicated evaluation of the missionary enterprise, lays the unavoidable impact of the supernatural. As more and more accounts of dream- and vision-enabled Muslim conversions are made public, a tentative question has found itself on the lips of many. After nearly 1,400 years of inter-religious conflict and remarkably little to show for the concerted missiological efforts directed at Muslims, is the phenomenon of dreams and visions an indication that a new grace-enabled tool has been brought to bear on the gospel witness directed toward the followers of Islam?

⸙⸙⸙⸙⸙

POINTS TO PONDER

1. How did early encounters between Islam and Christianity affect Muslim-Christian relations into the modern era?

2. To what does history ascribe the change in Christian attitudes toward Islam from the 12th to 13th centuries? How has what happened then been instrumental for missions in general in the following centuries?

3. What are some of the elements that handicapped mission efforts to Muslims from the 13th to 19th centuries? To what extent are these same handicaps affecting missions today?

4. What evidence is there that Muslims are responding more readily to the Christian message today than in the past?

5. To what can you attribute this change in responsiveness?

CHAPTER 4

Muslims Find Hope and Peace in Jesus

I once was lost but now am found, was blind but now I see.
—John Newton

But to all who believed Him and accepted Him, He gave the right to become children of God. They are reborn—not with a physical birth resulting from human passion or plan, but a birth that comes from God. —John 1:12-13 NLT

The following are true stories told to me by friends and acquaintances. Their experiences are examples of what is happening worldwide.

AISHA FINDS HOPE

With head bowed and a heavy heart, I said good-bye to Ali. He was leaving…again. And like the last time and the time before that, I had no idea how long he would be away. As I closed the door and shuffled back toward the living room of our small, unremarkable apartment in an un-important section of a large city in the Middle East, I was already lonely. I had no idea how I was going to cope all alone with the kids in the days and weeks and maybe months to come…alone. I had no idea.

My husband and I lived with our four kids in the same town in which I had grown up. And though I had made many friends in my 30-plus years, and though my sisters and brothers and their families as well as our parents all lived nearby, I felt alone…achingly, frustratingly, fearfully alone. The best I could tell, this loneliness was somehow linked to my husband, Ali.

Ali was not a bad man. He was not inattentive or selfish or abusive like many of the husbands of my friends. He cared for me and for our kids. He provided for us the best he knew how. And that was the problem, for in trying to provide for us, Ali had to leave to find work—leave not just our neighborhood or city, he had to leave our country for months at a time. The moment he left on these purposeful, caring adventures to provide for us, the crushing loneliness would weigh me down.

Without Ali, I felt unable to care for the needs of our four children. Gratefully none of them had any special needs. Though they were young, each one applied him or herself to their studies. They weren't rebellious, each one helped when they could, where they could. They missed their father too, and frankly, they understood even less why their father had to go away and for how long. At times the loneliness was nearly more than I could bear and often I would close myself in our bedroom, hoping the kids would not hear my weeping or my crying out to God—whoever and wherever He was—to bring Ali back, to help Ali find a job, to provide for the needs of the family. For in addition to my loneliness, the anxiety of having no stable income weighed heavily on my heart. And when I wasn't wondering where Ali was and what he was doing and when he could be coming home, I worried about how to pay rent and how I would be able to feed the kids.

One of the friends that Ali and I had made over the years was a family of Christians who lived across the street from us. This family had moved into the city some 12 years earlier and we had been the ones to help them to get settled in, show them where to shop, where to go get a flat tire fixed, who to call to get a telephone installed, and all the other things that neighbors do to welcome newcomers.

Over the years of this friendship, Ali and I had received a number of gifts from these Christians. One day we opened a package and found a copy of a film about the life of the Prophet Jesus. Another time it was a Bible, in Arabic. We were particularly fascinated by this gift as we were convinced that the Bible was for Westerners and so we never expected to see one in Arabic!

Each time Ali had been away, I found myself drawn more and more often to the friendship of these Christians and spent time nearly every week with them discussing the issues of life and faith. At first I was somewhat reluctant to talk about religious things with these friends knowing that they were Christians and my family and I were Muslims. I figured that because they believed so differently from me that there could be nothing that we could talk about that would not end in some kind of disagreement or worse. And I didn't need that, not with Ali gone. This time, perhaps more than ever before, I needed all the friendship that I could get. But that's not at all how it went. Our friends welcomed my questions about their Christian faith, and in return I did my best to answer theirs about Islam. But oh, how I wished Ali was home; he knew so much more than I did and would do a much better job helping our friends understand.

One night after having discussed spiritual things with our Christian friends, I had a dream. In my dream I saw a Man full of light. As I looked at Him, drawn by His strange but fabulous brightness, He spoke to me and told me that I should go across the street and ask the "brothers at the church" what I should do to become a "follower." When I awoke, the dream was still vividly etched in my consciousness. I was startled by it all and wondered what it could mean. Who was the Man in the dream? Who were the "brothers at the church"? And what did He mean by becoming a "follower"—a follower of whom? I decided to ignore it and not tell anyone.

Three or four days later, I had the same dream. Again, a brightly illuminated Man appeared to me. Again He spoke and told me to go across the street and ask the "brothers at the church" what I should do to become a "follower." This time I felt compelled to do something about it. Feeling certain that the Man in the dream must have been Jesus—the same Jesus I had seen in the film that my friends had given me and that I had been reading about in my Bible—I felt awed and strangely reassured. For some reason I was convinced that our Christian friends across the street must know who the "brothers at the church" must be, even though I had never met them.

With courage and uncertainty battling for first place in my heart, I made my way across the street to the apartment of our Christian friends and told them about the dream. I told them about the Man in shining white and what He said to me. And I asked them to contact the brothers from the church so that they could come and tell me what I should do to become a follower.

My friends contacted the church and arranged at time for me to meet with the brothers from the church. When we met, I excitedly retold to them the dream, doing my best to adequately describe the illuminated Man and recount what He told me, being careful to forget anything. In response, the brothers from the church opened their Bibles and explained to me the gospel of Jesus Christ. They encouraged me to read Scripture for myself and to ask God to help me understand who He was and what He wanted me to do. I was thrilled. As I read, I began to understand about Jesus, the One sent from God to take away my sin. I saw in the Bible how Jesus cared for people, healing some, feeding others, and always speaking in love to those who had needs.

The brothers from the church explained to me that Jesus was inviting me to become a follower of Him and that I could do so simply by admitting my sin and asking God for forgiveness. They added that Jesus could be counted on to help me in my loneliness and also that He would hear my cries for help, whenever and wherever I needed Him. And this is what I did. Throughout my life I had been a Muslim, trying to keep the rules and traditions of the faith. I had married a Muslim man, and God had given us four children. But now, it was as if all of life was turning over, starting over, and for the first time in a long time, I felt safe, loved, and light-hearted.

In the days and weeks that followed, I felt an unsatisfied craving to read the Bible and other books that our Christian friends loaned to me that talked about spiritual things. The more I read, the more I learned. The more I learned, the more I was eager to read. And the less lonely I felt.

After some months' time, I received news from my husband that he was coming home. I was overjoyed; at last after all this time, he was coming back to share life with me and our children. But then the thought seized me—what would Ali think of my new Christian faith? Would he be angry? Would he divorce me? Would he take the kids and really leave me all alone? As I waited for Ali's return, these questions turned over and over in my mind.

When Ali finally returned home to the excited and relieved greetings and affection of our family, he too was overjoyed. As the readjustment to one another wore on in the days that followed Ali couldn't help but notice my renewed vigor and light-heartedness. He watched me but said nothing, thinking that it must be due to his return and our reuniting as a family. One day he found my Bible, and then he knew: I had been reading it and I had decided to follow the faith of the Christians. That evening Ali took me aside and told me, "I understand now why you are smiling and happy. You are a Christian. I am Muslim, but I think I need to become a better Muslim so that I can continue to respond to your faith."

My life was changed by a dream—a dream of a Man who told me where to go and whom to ask to find out what I should do to become a follower; and not a follower of just anyone, but of Jesus. Despite my Muslim faith and family life, despite my loneliness and anxiety over the care for my family, I found hope, peace, and joy by heeding the voice of the Man in my dream.

༄༅༷༄༅

Miriam Finds Peace

The 1990s were difficult in Algeria. The cancelled elections in '92 and resultant clashes between private and political representatives made life hard—evenly deadly—for the Kabyle minority who were often targeted. In the midst of these trying times, I was often troubled by fear for myself, for my brothers, for my friends. In an effort to find hope, I began to pray, but not as before. This time I prayed for protection and comfort to Jesus just like the Man in the film I had recently seen.

But life was not only frightening for me, my entire family was feeling the effects of the hardship caused by the political turmoil. The first to "escape" was my uncle, who, in 1992, left Algeria for France with the intention of applying for asylum as a political refugee. With his departure from the house, I had access to his bedroom where I discovered a treasure trove of books and one in particular—the Bible! Amazed and thrilled by my discovery of the Christian Scriptures, I began to read them with wonder and expectation. *What a coincidence,* I thought, *that the very same year I would become the first in my family to get serious and investigate the teachings of Islam and to begin to practice the prayer ritual common to the faith, that I would also find a Bible.*

I turned at first to the Book of Genesis but didn't read far before getting bogged down in the unfamiliar stories, and I found myself skipping to other parts of the Bible hoping to find something more interesting. Soon I discovered the Psalms and Proverbs. The more I read of these, the more I felt a connection to their message. Over the following months, amidst the turmoil that raged in Algeria, and especially in the Kabyle region, I turned time and again to the words of the Psalms for comfort.

A year later, in 1993, my grandfather left for France to undergo an operation. While in the hospital, someone gave him a copy of the Jesus film in his native tongue—Kabyle. He was overjoyed to finally have a copy of a film in his mother tongue, as far as he knew, the *only* film in Kabyle at the time. Grandfather longed to return to Algeria to show it to us all. As soon as his hospital stay was over, Grandfather returned to Algeria with the film, excited by the possibility of showing it to the whole family. I still remember the day shortly after Grandfather's return when I along with all my brothers and sisters and cousins piled into Grandfather's bedroom to watch the Jesus film on the only videocassette player in the home.

I remember I was deeply touched by the film and especially by the person of Jesus. At the end of the film, there is a scene in which a narrator appears and explains the purpose of Jesus' life and death on the cross and then leads in prayer. Hearing the prayer in Kabyle was deeply significant for me. I had never heard anyone pray like that in Kabyle before. I was riveted by the words, which seemed to express the deepest feelings of my heart. For a long time afterward the memory of that prayer and those words burned in my heart.

Time passed and I eventually made my way through the rest of the Old Testament. Eventually I found the New Testament and the Gospels. As I read, I couldn't help but recall the events surrounding the life and person of Jesus—the Jesus I had seen in the film. Reading the words took me back to the scenes of the film, and I could almost hear Jesus talking and see Him walking.

One day while crossing through the center of our town, I saw an old friend from high school who, to my great surprise, was preaching the Christian message in the public square! I couldn't believe it! I didn't remember this guy to have been a Christian when we were in high school together. I wondered what had happened to him…and why he was putting himself in danger by speaking so openly about Jesus. Didn't he realize that this was a Muslim country?! I stood at a distance so I could hear him but not too close in case someone saw me listening.

He must have recognized me for afterward he came running up to me calling out my name. We talked. He asked me what I thought about what he said. I didn't say much, because I really wasn't sure. He seemed to say some of the same things that I had heard in the movie and that I had read in the Bible. But I wasn't sure. He gave me a book, the Gospel of John, part of the New Testament of the Christian Scriptures, he explained. And then he invited me to his church. A church? In my town? In Algeria?

Although my family was pretty "open" in the sense that my parents were not overly strict about clothing and Islamic rituals, and although I had this irresistible urge to go and see what it was all about, I knew that going to a Christian church with some guy from high school was not going to be possible! But I did read the Gospel of John that he gave me, and again I was deeply touched by the life and words of Jesus.

In 2000, I made my own way to France in an effort to leave the difficult circumstances of Algeria behind. Without papers and without a stable living situation, life was hard. One afternoon, I was invited to the apartment of one of my aunt's who lived in Paris. Thrilled to be included, I accepted the invitation and was glad to meet a number of neighbors and my aunt's friends. At one point in the afternoon, one of the ladies, Elaine, bowed her head and appeared to pray before she ate. I was surprised—we never do anything like that in Islam! I wondered if she was a Christian. I watched her for a time and after struggling with what to say, I finally rustled up the courage to ask her if she was a Christian. Elaine said that she was and then, surprise, she asked me the same thing! What was I going to say now! I fumbled, stuttered, and not wanting to appear rude, told her that I believed in Jesus! My aunt must have overheard the conversation because when I looked over in her direction her face was screwed up into an expression of shock!

To avoid making a scene, I motioned for this lady to follow me into the hallway where I was able to show her the copy of the Gospel of John that I carried with me everywhere I went since the day that my high school friend had given it to me. Elaine was very pleased and invited me to come with her to church the following Sunday.

Some months later, Ramadan—the month of prescribed Islamic fasting—began. I had by now been to the church several times with my new friend, Elaine. I still read the copy of the Gospel of John that I carried with me everywhere I went. I still turned to the Psalms and prayed in Jesus' name when I felt afraid. But for some reason, I began feeling troubled, overwhelmed by doubts with regard to the Christian things I had been reading and to which I was feeling increasingly attracted. In my confusion, I decided to follow the fasting regimen of Ramadan.

The following Sunday, in keeping with the tradition of the church, a meal was organized for all who had come. Because I was keeping the fast of Ramadan, I couldn't share in the meal, and so I tried to slip quietly out the back door, hoping that no one would notice me. But just as I was going out the door, Elaine caught me by the arm and asked why I wasn't staying to eat with everyone. I didn't want to hide anything—least of all from Elaine—and so I admitted that I was feeling unsure about all this Christian "stuff" and that I had begun to follow Ramadan. I guess I was expecting Elaine to react in some way and perhaps tell me how bad I was or how bad Islam was. But she didn't. It's like she wasn't even surprised. Instead of the shock and rebuke that I expected from her, Elaine encouraged me to pray and ask the God of Creation to reveal Himself to me. Surprised and encouraged by Elaine's kind and wise response, I spent each of the next three evenings on my knees praying to the God of Creation, asking Him to reveal Himself to me.

On the third night, after praying and falling asleep, I had a dream. In my dream, I found myself in the midst of a huge room, like a stadium with a covered roof. The stadium was filled with people of every race and of every age: adults, children, babies, and grandparents. As I looked around and tried to take in the sights and sounds of the crowd, I felt alone and a little lost. After a few minutes an older woman came up to me and said, "You look like you're a little lost." I replied that indeed I was. And then I asked the older women who she was, who all these people were, and what was happening. As the woman talked, I noticed in the center of the room a line of people leading to a Person standing in front of a large desk, dressed in what looked like the robes of a judge. As I watched the Judge, from time to time He would open a door and the person in front of Him would go through it and leave the stadium. Other times the Judge would gesture to the person in front of Him to leave. Puzzled by this, I asked the woman what was happening with the people in the line. The woman replied, "If you want to find out, you have to get in line." So, I did.

I waited patiently for my turn to face the Judge. When I finally did so, I noticed indeed that He was standing in front of a large and beautiful desk. Behind the desk was a huge bookshelf full of beautifully bound books the titles of which were written in gold letters. On the desk in front of me I noticed three large books. On one was written, "Holy Bible" and on another, "Holy Koran." The third book I did not recognize.

Seeing the Koran I remarked to the Judge, "I see that you have the Koran." And the Judge replied, "I have respect for true Muslims." And then He added that it was up to me to choose one of the books. I at first felt drawn to the Koran as it reminded me of Algeria and the faith that I had become familiar with as a teenager. But suddenly and inexplicably, I picked up the Bible instead. At that moment, the Judge said, "I am proud of your choice. Now you can enter by the door." With these words, the Judge turned and opened the door. As He did so, I was struck by an overwhelming scene full of warmth and brightness that filled the space beyond the door through which I was entering. The next thing I remember was waking from my dream with a great sense of joy and peace knowing that I had made the right choice.

Convinced by the dream that the Bible and its message were true, I stopped following Ramadan. The next Sunday I went to the church this time with a renewed energy and expectation. I found my friend Elaine and excitedly told her about my dream—the stadium filled with people, the Judge, the books, the door, my choice, and the joy and peace that I felt. Elaine was thrilled. Over the next couple of weeks, she helped me understand the significance of the symbols in the dream. And then again I prayed, this time asking Jesus to forgive my sins and fill my life.

ᴑᵻᴑᵻᴑᵻᴑ

AMINA'S STORY

Loneliness. If there was ever one word that summed up my life that was it. I'm not exactly sure why I felt so lonely, for in a way, I was happy. I had a husband. I had a daughter. I had a home. My husband never mistreated me and he never asked me what I did or where I went. As long as he had what he needed, all was well. And yet, everywhere I went I felt lonely. When I talked with my friends or sisters, they told me about their husbands and the way they did things together; about the family project to build a house or take a vacation together. I couldn't help but compare my life with theirs, and I was saddened. It's as if I was longing for something more, and I didn't really know what.

My husband, the Imam, was a very disciplined and religious man. Every day he would rise early and go to the mosque. In the evening he returned home to eat and go to bed. His religious devotion disappointed me as he rarely participated in society outside of the function of the mosque. He didn't attend weddings or parties of our friends or family, he didn't go on outings, he didn't take time out just to be with me and our daughter. Interestingly, he allowed me to participate in all of these things and even go on my own to visit friends or family as I wished—as long as I was home in time to prepare the evening meal. Sometimes I wondered if this was all there was to life.

Amid the loneliness that haunted my days, sometime during those early married years, a question began to roll around in my mind: *What happens to me when I die?* For some reason I had this feeling that I was not prepared for death. I was afraid that because I didn't always tell the truth that somehow this was going to affect what happened to me after I died. My conscience was working overtime to make me feel guilty about my lying, but I felt that it would be impossible to live by only telling the truth. Lying was part of life. I did it. My family did it. Everyone did it. But something about it seemed wrong.

In 1990, my daughter married and moved to Belgium. Over the next couple of years I would periodically visit, staying up to three months at a time. In 1995, my daughter's husband left her, and I moved to Belgium to live with and help my daughter with her three small children. Then my daughter began seeing a man from Holland who was from a nominal Christian background. When she told me about him and his family's religious background, I was anxious but consoled myself with the thought that if they were nominal Christians and not fanatical, then perhaps religion wouldn't play an important role in their lives. But what I really feared was my daughter being obliged to change her faith if she were to marry this man.

In reality I was not very religious myself. As a child, it was my mother and not my father who was the religious one of the family. Like most children from Morocco, we followed our mother's influence when it came to religious matters and learned and practiced our Islamic faith the way she did. But apart from keeping Ramadan, my eight brothers and sisters and I did little else to show our faith.

When I was 12 or 13 years of age, I became acquainted with some neighbors who were from Spain. According to my father, these neighbors were Christians and, like the Jews, had their own religion and their own book, the Bible. I was intrigued by them and would sometimes go to watch them pray and listen to them sing. My father thought they were nice people, upright and trustworthy. My mother, however, warned me about spending too much time with them, afraid that they might turn me away from our Muslim faith. When I married at the age of 16 to a local Imam, I lost all contact with these Christian neighbors, but I never completely forgot the sound of their prayers and the joy of their music. Little did I know that this Christian faith would come to be my own one day.

On one occasion after my daughter had been seeing this nominal Christian man for some time, she and I were approached in the metro by two Jehovah Witnesses. In response to their questions about us and our religious background, I was surprised to hear my daughter telling them about Jesus Christ. I didn't realize that she knew so much about Him and that she was able to so effectively respond to their questions. It was obvious to me that the faith of this new boyfriend was beginning to take shape in the mind of my daughter. What surprised me even more was the fact that my daughter invited these two women to come by our apartment later that afternoon to talk further!

When the women arrived later that afternoon, they immediately offered us a Bible in Arabic. I eagerly accepted it as I was thrilled to see a Bible in my maternal Arabic language. The conversation between these women and my daughter took off in French which, though I understood for the most part, left me unable to respond. I heard a lot that morning about God and His love. When they talked about Jesus being the Son of God, I couldn't stand it. That idea went against a direct teaching of Islam. I gave back the Bible and went into another room.

My daughter followed me into the room and asked me why I was upset. I explained to her that I didn't appreciate what they were saying about Jesus and God. I told her that if she insisted in talking with them that I would kick them out of the apartment myself, and that if they were ever to come back, then I would leave. It was either them or me! When they left, I refused to say good-bye. Unknown to me, they left the Bible. My daughter hid it away, fearing that I would get angry if I found it and started to read it.

As the relationship between my daughter and this nominal Christian man developed, I reluctantly realized that they were heading toward marriage. I eventually told my daughter that it would be fine with me if she married him. I really just wanted my daughter to be happy, after all, and I told myself that if this man makes her happy, then I didn't want to stand in the way. But in reality, I was hoping that the relationship would end. I didn't like the idea of my daughter changing her religion because of a husband. Why her?

Everyone in our family was Muslim: grandfathers and grandmothers, aunts and uncles, brothers and sisters. Why should she be the one to change and leave us? The more I thought about it, the angrier I became. When the time finally came for her to leave Belgium and move to Sweden to marry him, I remember saying good-bye to her in the airport and saying to myself, *When she comes back for a visit, I will confront her and tell her it is either Jesus or me. If she wants to be a Christian with this new husband of hers, she can have him; but I will no longer live with or visit her.*

All that night, I couldn't sleep. I was consumed by anger and worry over what would happen to my daughter. The next day, I worked around the house in anger as I wrestled with the same thoughts. At some point near evening, while I was sitting on the couch in the living room, my thoughts turned into some sort of prayer to I'm not sure who. And in this "prayer" I said, "If Islam is right, then I will do everything—pray five times a day and even fast during Ramadan in a disciplined and pure way—to put a stop to this marriage. But if Christianity is right, then God you are going to have to show me." After I prayed, I sent my other children off to their rooms for the night and slumped back onto the couch.

Then suddenly, at the end of the hallway, I saw a white light and white-robed Man standing there with a shepherd's staff in His hand that reached from the floor to the ceiling. I thought at first that the light must have been some sort of reflection from an outside light onto the television screen. I turned off the television but the light remained. I gazed at the Man bathed in the incredibly white light, whiter than I had ever seen. He stood there without speaking for what seemed like a long time.

Somehow I knew it to be Jesus, though I had never seen Him before. In the quietness, with the hallway and living room bathed in a brilliant white light, a tremendous sense of peace filled the house. A few minutes later, my daughter called me from Sweden. I told her that Jesus was with me in the house, right now! Immediately she went to tell her husband who in turn assured me that Jesus was calling me to come to Him. But what did that mean? I had no idea what he was talking about. All night long I felt Jesus standing in the hallway surrounded by the bright light. In the morning when I woke, He was gone; but for the next two nights, He came and stood in the hallway, never speaking, just standing still with the long white staff. After the third night, Jesus didn't come back. I looked for Him but I couldn't find Him.

A couple of weeks later, my daughter came for a visit. As soon as I saw her, I told her I wanted to know who Jesus was. She told me that she had hidden away some booklets and the copy of the Arabic Bible; hidden she said, because she had been afraid that I would be angry if I had known that she had them. She ran to get them and then began to tell me about Jesus. When she spoke of Him, I felt a kind of joy mingled with peace welling up inside of me. As I listened to her speak, and as I read the booklets and some of the Bible, something began to shift in my thinking. I didn't know if I was becoming convinced of Jesus and the Christian way or not. I liked the stories of the Old Testament prophets because many were the same that we revered in Islam. The more I read, the more I wanted to read.

In addition to the books and the Bible, my daughter also gave me the phone number of a church in Brussels. She invited me to go with her, but I refused. I thought that a church was a big huge cathedral full of crucifixes and other things that were contrary to my Muslim faith. But what was worse, I feared that if I did go someone who knew me would see me. Despite my refusal, my daughter called the pastor of the church several times and talked with him. Finally she went. When she returned, she told me about what happened and about the people she met. What surprised me more than anything else was the fact that she met other Arab ladies there at the church! After much encouragement from my daughter, I finally said yes, and went with her to a weekly ladies Bible study at the church. I liked it. The people were warm and friendly. The story from the Bible was interesting. Something was drawing me again to this Jesus.

That night, after attending the Bible study at the church earlier in the day, I had a dream. I dreamed that I was back home in Morocco and looking down a long street toward my maternal home. Suddenly I was standing in front of my house all alone; no one else was in the street. As I looked around at the other houses across the street, I noticed that the sky was grey but growing brighter and turning white. When I looked up, I saw Someone in blazing white descending from the sky dressed in traditional Moroccan clothes. The Man continued descending until He came to stand behind me.

And then He spoke, "I am the Lord. I have forgiven all of your sins." I turned and saw Him kneeling down and tracing out white squares in the dirt. I watched Him for a time; the tracings of the squares puzzled me. After a while He said, "These squares represent the houses that I am preparing in Heaven for those who believe in Me. Those who accept and speak My words, they will dwell here."

Suddenly I was taken in my dream back to Belgium and I found myself standing in front of the entrance to a hammam (traditional Turkish bath). As I stood outside wondering if I should go in, I had the sensation of waking from my dream and the thought came to mind, *If I tell anyone about this, who is going to believe me?* And with that question on my lips, I felt compelled to go in. Inside the front door, I saw a well covered by a white arch. I felt cold however, so I went into the next room. Still feeling cold, I continued to pass through room after room in an attempt to find one that was warm.

Finally I came to a warm room surrounding a huge, white bathtub full to the brim with warm water. I decided to stay. Somehow without going into the bath, I felt as if I was being washed. It felt different this time, deeper and cleaner. When I finished, I was given a white towel and then I saw Jesus sitting on a stool, dressed in a robe and with sandals on His feet. I said to myself, "If this is Jesus, then He is the only One who can explain what my dreams mean and convince me that He is the Son of God."

I sat down next to Him and looked at His feet. I began to tell Him about my dreams and the Man with the shepherd's staff in my apartment and the Man descending out of Heaven near my home in Morocco. I told Him that the Man said that He was the Lord and that He had forgiven my sins. He listened and didn't say anything. When I looked up, I saw that He was smiling at me and looking into my eyes.

Then I woke up. I felt joy that I had never known; joy that I had never felt in my whole life. I went into the kitchen and my daughter noticed that my face was radiating with joy. She asked me what was different, and I said, "Oh, nothing." She insisted, "Mother, I have never seen you this happy ever, tell me what happened." So I did. I told her about the dreams, about the Man in white who descended out of Heaven, about the hammam and meeting Jesus inside it. And I told her how everything was always so white and pure next to Jesus. Immediately she called her husband and told him what I had seen. He said, "In our family, we grew up reading about Jesus and going to church. In some way Jesus was familiar to us. But you, coming as you have from Islam, have had the privilege of seeing Jesus face to face."

The last of these dreams took place in July 2000. Following the dreams, I began attending the church where I met the Arab ladies. One day while at home, I called out to God, thanking Him for having revealed Himself to me in these dreams. I confessed to Him my sins and asked Him to forgive me and make me His follower. In December 2000, I was baptized and gave public testimony of my faith in Jesus Christ, the Man in white, the One who had forgiven all my sin.

ༀ❖ༀ❖ༀ❖

Points to Ponder

1. Describe the life circumstances of Aisha. How did her situation prepare her to respond to her dream experience?

2. What elements contributed to Miriam's response to her dream experience?

3. Amina's story describes her initial attraction to and later opposition to Christianity that was ultimately overturned as a result of a dream and vision encounter with Christ. How did these two supernatural events respond to her fears and anti-Christian feelings?

4. How was the symbolism of the white light, white robes, white bath, etc., significant for her? What did the whiteness of things symbolize for her? Why was this significant?

5. How did the Christian friends of Aisha, Miriam, and Amina play significant roles in helping them leave Islam for faith in Christ?

CHAPTER 5

Exploring the Supernatural World

It was six men of Indostan
To learning much inclined,
Who went to see the Elephant
(Though all of them were blind),
That each by observation,
Might satisfy his mind.

The Blind Men and the Elephant
by John Godfrey Saxe

He replied, "You are permitted to understand the secrets of the
Kingdom of God. But I use parables to teach the others so that
the Scriptures might be fulfilled: When they look, they won't
really see. When they hear, they won't understand." —Jesus,
Luke 8:10 NLT

Day after day, the middle-aged Muhammad, husband-merchant of the wealthy Khadija, retreated to Mount Hira just outside the Arabian desert city of Mecca to contemplate his life. One evening, in the vast solitude of his surroundings, a shocking, angelic vision changed his life, and that of the Arab peoples, forever. Sura 53 of the Qur'an records the event as follows:

By the Star when it goes down, your Companion is neither astray nor being misled, nor does he say (aught) of (his own) Desire. It is no less than inspiration sent down to him: He was taught by one mighty in Power, endued with Wisdom: for he appeared (in stately form) while he was in the highest part of the horizon: Then he approached and came closer, and it was at a distance of but two bow-lengths or (even) nearer; So did (Allah) convey the inspiration to His Servant (Conveyed) what He (meant) to convey. The (Prophet's) (mind and) heart in no way falsified that which he saw. Will ye then dispute with him concerning what he saw? For indeed he saw him at a second descent, Near the Lote-tree of the utmost boundary. Near it is the Garden of Abode.[1]

Muhammad was so distressed by this episode that he feared he had encountered a jinn[2] and that he might, as a result of this incident and against his wishes, become one of the much-aligned soothsayers of his day. Yet through the counsel of a cousin and his wife, Khadija, Muhammad gradually began to view this event as a divinely orchestrated exercise designed to set him apart as a prophet of Allah.[3]

ANGELIC VISIONS

According to the recorded history and traditions of his life, Muhammad had a second angelic vision nearly three years later. Similar to the first vision, Muhammad was instructed to recite (record) the words conveyed by the angelic being, Gabriel.[4] These incidents, exceptional as they were in that no other similar vision experiences are recorded throughout the remainder of Muhammad's life,[5] served as the inception of the Qur'an and the birth of the Islamic faith.

Because this incident marks the beginnings of Islam, it is obviously highly regarded by its adherents. The theological conclusions that resulted from this supernatural encounter including man's relationship to God, the means and nature of revelation, and the mark or identity of a prophet have become foundational to the Islamic faith. Of particular interest is the means and nature of revelation that resulted in the Qur'an (Koran). According to the *Concise Encyclopedia of Islam*:

...the theory of the revelation of the Koran is particularly complex. The Koran was revealed or descended in its entirety in one night, the 'Night of Destiny,' into the soul of the Prophet (Muhammad), which is itself that night. Thereupon it became manifest through him, in segments, sometimes entire surahs, as particular circumstances and requirements in the world and the Prophet's life called them forth. The Prophet said that this manifestation of the Koran came in two ways: "Sometimes Gabriel reveals to me as one man to anther, and that is easy; but at other times it is like the ringing of bell penetrating my very heart, rending me, and that way is the most painful."[6]

Thus revelation, and its common vehicle dreams and visions, are inseparably united in the worldview of Islam which, since its rather abrupt beginnings, has continued to benefit from supernatural[7] guidance gleaned from such phenomena. In a worldview that embraces that "faith is conviction through direct experience, and not the result of a process of reason,"[8] the dreams and visions play a significant role in informing and defining religious meaning. In contrast to Western thought, which has historically given little credence to the unconscious, Muslims are fully aware of and engaged in a daily experience that is not only open to, but depends upon supernatural encounters such as occur in dreams and visions. For Muslims:

> ...dreams are central to the cosmological outlook of ordinary Muslims from founder to followers, dreams form part of the total paradigm within which Muslims live and move, touch and are touched, meet and are met. They are not optional; they are a meaningful component of life.[9]

Not only are dreams and visions considered to be vehicles of divine communication, but Mohammad himself noted that though his death would signal the end of Koranic revelation, God would continue to reveal Himself through dreams and visions to the Muslim community. In this way then, dreams and visions have become a successor of sorts to the revealed Koranic message. As such, dream interpretation, for the Muslim, serves as a form of unmediated access to God.[10]

Following the eventual death of the prophet and the ending of Koranic revelation, dreams and visions grew in importance as means of hearing directly from God. As a result, the science of dream interpretation developed and prompted the compilation of interpretation manuals to assist in decoding the meanings of recurring symbols in the dream and vision events. What is remarkable is to what extent these dream manuals played a role in the religious life of the Muslim in the succeeding centuries following the death of Mohammad—an indication of just how prominent the phenomenon of dreams and visions had become.

Lamoreaux remarks, "…to judge from the number of dream manuals alone, one would have to conclude that the interpretation of dreams was as important to these Muslims as the interpretation of the Koran. Some sixty dream manuals were composed during the first four and a half centuries of the Muslim era. During that same period, very nearly exactly the same number of Koranic commentaries were composed."[11] Clearly, dreams and visions played a central role in Muslim religious life. A historical review of the development of the rise of interpretation manuals and dream experts leads us to conclude that for a Muslim, "…to reject dream interpretation, is to reject the Prophet and his commands. …it is [therefore] incumbent on good Muslims to attend to their dreams and their prophetic significance."[12]

DREAMS AND VISIONS DEFINED

However, despite the importance afforded the incidence of dreams and visions in Islam, it does not clearly distinguish between them. The Arabic words commonly used to refer to these experiences do not provide for explicit categories. For instance, the word *ru'ya* literally means "vision." However, Sura 48:27 states, "God has already fulfilled in truth the dream [vision, *'ar-ru'ya*] for His Prophet…." Here the term may mean either "vision" or, most likely, a "prophetic dream" indicating God's provision or activity on behalf of the prophet before the events occurred in reality.[13]

A second Arabic term used in this context is *tanzil*. Though the word literally means, "a sending down [from Heaven]," its implicit reference to the revelation of the Qur'an to Muhammad, endows it with a much broader meaning suggestive of the dream and vision revelatory event.[14]

The third common Arabic term used in reference to dreams and visions is *al-Wahy*. This word denotes "inspiration from God," and, like the term *tanzil*, is suggestive of not only the content of revelation, but of the means and process as well.[15]

From the Arabic terms used to describe the revelatory process carried by dreams and visions, it is apparent that distinction between the types and/or means of the revelatory process is not as important as the event itself. Therefore, despite the fact that dreams and visions appear to be unique types of experiences differentiated by the state of sleep of the subject, the understanding of such a distinction in the Muslim worldview is not clearly evident.

Throughout the Muslim world, dreams serve a variety of societal functions. For instance, among the Tausag of the Philippines, medicine men begin their "medical" practice through dreams in which they are visited by shayatin (devils). In Afghan Turkestan, the bakhshi (doctor) will spend the night sleeping in the house of a patient. The dream received during the night becomes the key to diagnosing the patient's illness and defining the appropriate treatment. The Kaybles of Algeria put food on the graves of deceased relatives if they dream of them, in an effort to communicate with them. In Pakistan, the shrines of dead saints are established as the direct result of dreams, especially as the details of such are revealed in the dreams of recognized holy men.[16]

Formal and Folk Islam

But if dreams and visions are so popular among Muslims and serve as a primary means of revelation, how are they to be understood in terms of Muslim theology? In answer to this question, one must look to literature, which is for the most part external to Islam that divides the generally monolithic orthodoxy of Islam from its popular and culturally varied expressions of the faith. The former is referred to as "formal" or "official" Islam, whereas the latter is known as "popular" or "folk" Islam.

Formal Islam embodies the official doctrines and practice of the Islamic faith that are accepted across the Muslim world. Included are such things as the Five Pillars,[17] the recognized festivals, and reverence and study of the

Qur'an. Formal Islam holds to and presents God as the Creator but who is functionally removed from His creation—what some might call "deistic." By virtue of its dependence and the Qur'an as the primary text of doctrinal instruction, formal Islam deals with the universal issues of life such as origins, destiny, and the true meaning of life. Finally, formal Islam is what is taught in the Quranic schools and centers of religious training that prepare men for roles as Imams and Islamic scholars and teachers across the Muslim world.

In contrast, popular, or folk Islam, encompasses the myriad of colloquial beliefs and practices of Muslims that, in addition to the Five Pillars and other formal aspects of the faith, are intended to give meaning and counsel in the daily course of life. Because God is understood to be far off and uninvolved in the immediate affairs of men, folk Islam draws upon local beliefs and practices to respond to the pressing, daily needs, and provide answers to the challenges and fears of living in a hostile world. Unlike the commonly held beliefs and practices that fall under formal Islam, the beliefs and practices of folk Islam are not codified and taught in formal settings. They are instead handed down from generation to generation and as such vary widely from region to region and even from family to family.

Another way of categorizing the differences between the two types or realms of Islamic faith is in terms of "need"; formal Islam addresses the religious needs, whereas folk Islam addresses the felt needs of the Muslim.

Though Islam is largely regarded as an orthodoxy marked by ritual adherence to the five duties or pillars previously mentioned, a far-reaching reliance upon unconscious, supernatural phenomena demonstrates that at the heart of its orthopraxy (adherence to ethical and liturgical conduct) is a lifestyle saturated with superstition within which dreams and visions play a significant role. This dualism is however, not simply a chaotic reaction to formal religion as expressed in Islam. Rather it is a trans-religious existential attempt to apply religious meaning to the ordinary events and circumstances of life.

As Bill Musk observes in his treatment of the aspects of folk Islam, "in every expression of monotheistic faith (which includes Islam) a gap has developed, almost inevitably, between faith as defined theologically and faith as it finds expression in ordinary people's lives."[18]

Musk continues his analysis of the propensity to create a religious dynamism by noting that this gap between doctrine and daily living tends to be more pronounced in those faiths in which God is depicted as deistic. It is as if those who live under the construct of a deistic faith are emotionally driven to "invent" a so-called "intermediate reality" because of their dissatisfaction with being out of touch with a deistic god. This intermediate reality is often filled with numerous categories of quasi-divine beings and superstitious rituals intended to give meaning to and answer the questions of the everyday routine of life.

Musk describes this intermediate reality as "trans-empirical by nature and operating in an otherworldly domain" although not necessarily always outside of the natural realm.[19] Because the primary tenets of Islam are built upon the dual understanding of the extreme transcendence of Allah and the ultimate submission of humankind, the Islamic faith becomes a natural breeding ground for intermediate, superstitious, and folk elements of which dreams and visions are primary.

Intermediate Realities

The more than one billion Muslims scattered over every major continent and defined by many different cultures and subcultures have inevitably nurtured the formation of untold numbers of varieties of these intermediate realities, which in turn find expression in various forms of Islamic ritual and belief. Some of these are products of a syncretism between animism or naturalism and Islam, and in addition to the tenets of Formal Islam, include reverence for certain objects, animals, or persons (dead or alive). For instance, miniature copies of the Qur'an or selected verses are pinned to the clothing of children and placed in the rear windows of cars as talismans throughout the Muslim world.[20] In this widespread practice, the Qur'an itself is believed to contain power to protect the wearer of the talisman from harm and sickness.

Other expressions of intermediate realities result from a merging of mysticism and Islam, and in addition to the tenets of formal Islam, include transcendental activities and the quest for new revelation. One popular expression of this union of formal Islam and mysticism is Sufism. *Sufism* is an entire branch of Islam:

> at the heart of which is the belief that one's self must die, that is, one must undergo annihilation (fana) of the lower, ego-centered self in order to abide or rest (baqa) in God.... The goal of the Sufi was a direct knowledge or personal religious experience of God's presence.[21]

Still other expressions of intermediate realities result from the union of local and/or tribal customs, pagan religions, and secularism brought together with the tenets of formal Islam. For example, in sub-Saharan Africa, as in much of the Muslim world, Muslim converts continue their ritual involvement in ancestor veneration in attempts to gain spiritual benefits.[22]

Though varied in their origins, these expressions of faith at the popular level nevertheless have much in common in that they all reflect an attempt by the "faithful" to make sense of the events and circumstances of daily life. Furthermore, in addition to giving meaning to the experiences and everyday routine, these unique local expressions of Islam also seek to provide a means of protection for the individual and community from evil or harm as administered by satan, the jinn, or God Himself. In an insightful summary, Musk elaborates on the importance of folk Islam to the ordinary Muslim:

> The worldview of popular Islam is built upon and integrates with the everyday stresses and joys of ordinary people. There is a lack of dissonance with the alternative, official Islamic worldview simply because the popular view of the world is more appropriate, more mundane and more pervasive. Without a dynamic, divine involvement, contradictory of its own systematic tenets, official Islam cannot hope to compete for the uncompromising patronization of most Muslims, for it cannot meet their most fundamental needs. Ideal (or Formal) Islam has few resources for dealing with the everyday concerns and nightly dreads of ordinary Muslims;

popular Islam, on the contrary, knows an abundance of remedies. Each local community recognizes practitioners who can provide charms or ceremonies necessary to affect peace of mind and to restore equilibrium.[23]

As a result, folk Islam through the practice and perpetuation of its locally defined rituals has become the dominant force in the lives of Muslims throughout the Islamic world. In fact, in many Islamic settings, some of these unwritten local (folk Islamic) practices and traditions, *adat*, "have the force of social law alongside Islamic law (shari'ah), and the civil code."[24] Because of the tangible, practical nature of such beliefs and practices, folk Islam serves as the framework within which the individual Muslim views the world, collects and processes information, and explains reality. So pervasive is the role of these mystical, natural, or animistic elements in Islam that, despite its deistic view of God and the necessity of adherence to the tenets of the formal faith, much of the religious element of the Muslim worldview has been established upon the basis that "faith is a conviction (that comes through) direct experience and not the result of a process of reason."[25] In light of this, it is evident that supernatural and superstitious phenomena, of which dreams and visions are a part, are prominent sources of religious significance for the Muslim.

An Inherent Cosmological Gap

And what does this mean for the Christian, and in particular a Western Christian, who desires to explain his faith to a Muslim? If the evaluation of the Muslim worldview provided above is accurate, then the Christian who desires to engage in evangelistic activity designed to bring Muslims to faith in Jesus Christ cannot afford to ignore the unique pattern of folk Islam adopted by his Muslim friend. For unless the Christian can explain to his Muslim friend the person of Christ and His finished work on the cross from within[26] the context of his particular folk Islamic worldview via the appropriate means, symbols, and language, the gospel may not be fully nor accurately understood and a genuine opportunity to hear and respond to the gospel cannot be said to have occurred.

Roland Muller, in his popular book, *Honor and Shame*, in which he describes the ease of miscommunication across worldviews, says:

> The danger comes, however, when we [that is those of us who hold primarily to a western worldview] take our Roman understanding of the Gospel and apply it to those who do not have a Roman-based culture. We fruitlessly spend untold hours and incalculable amounts of energy explaining to our contact that he is guilty of sin, and needs to be justified before God. The poor person, on the other hand, may not even have a word for sin, or perhaps even the concept of sin, in his language. He struggles to understand guilt, and sees no need for justification. When he doesn't respond, we label him as resistant. We feel good about having given the gospel, because we analyze our own efforts by the meaning of right and wrong (the dominant paradigm of the western worldview and the basis of the Roman understanding of the gospel), and if we did all the right things, and he did not respond, then he must be resistant.[27]

In contrast to the worldview of folk Islam, the Western worldview[28] elevates the role of the rational and logical and affords little credence to superstitious or supernatural phenomena. As Musk notes:

> …the normal cosmological map of the Westerner emphasizes a fairly strong distinction between the natural and supernatural worlds. 'God' operates in the realm of the supernatural, 'science' explains the events of the natural environment.[29]

Because "science" and its methodology have become so significant to the Western mind in defining reality and managing the drama of life, Westerners are predisposed to think and act in terms of a strong dichotomy between sacred and secular. As a result, the Western mind more readily accepts as true that which is repeatable and verifiable and mistrusts that which is not. The Muslim on the other hand, more readily accepts as true that which he can experience. It is evident then that when the Western-minded Christian approaches a Muslim whose worldview is dominated by folk Islam, an inherent cosmological gap must be bridged in order for real communication to take place.

So what's a Christian to do? How can he make himself understood to his Muslim friend? What is involved in appropriate communication that effectively bridges the worldview gap between the two? First, the Christian must understand the essentials of communication.

Effective Communication

Communication consists, in its simplest form, of three components: the source (who is communicating), the coded message (what is being communicated), and the respondent (the one(s) who receive the message).[30] Once he understands this, the Christian's task is to accurately formulate the message that he wishes to communicate; with appropriate content, making use of appropriate means, and having in mind his intended audience. Second, the Christian must accept the fact there are built-in obstacles to understanding his message. Though the evangelistic task is fundamentally one of communication, which is for all intents and purposes nothing more than "an elemental human activity," this fundamental evangelistic task also encounters "a fundamental human problem,"[31] which is the reality of differing worldviews.

So the Western Christian who intends to communicate the gospel to Muslims, for example, is automatically confronted with additional challenges, beyond that of preparing an effective message, which are not just cross-cultural in nature, but cross-worldview. These challenges include such things as competing understandings of truth, differing meanings of shared terms, and undefined concepts. And the reality is that if the Christian fails to grasp and respond effectively to these challenges, he cannot be sure that what he intended to communicate was understood. Therefore, if the Western-minded Christian is to truly communicate, he must encode his message in language and symbols that, when transmitted to his Muslim audience, are rightly received and decoded with the intended meaning.[32]

Because of its largely unrepeatable and unverifiable nature, supernatural phenomena, which include dreams and visions, are viewed skeptically and considered largely inconsequential to the rational, logic-oriented diagnosis and decision making of recent Western thought. Musk observes that, "To western thought, 'dream' connotes reverie rather than reality, imagination rather than objective truth, fancy rather than fact, misty vagueness rather than understanding."[33] And yet, as we have already seen, the Bible, in both the Old and New Testaments, record incidents in which dreams played a significant role in the lives of saints.

How are these incidents to be understood in our 21st century, modern setting? Though Western Christendom has often equated its worldview with that of the Bible, is it possible that the Western man's worldview has departed from, or at least fails to include, all that the biblical worldview entails? (Refer to Table 2 for a brief overview of biblical, Muslim, and Western worldviews.)

TABLE 2
COMPARISON OF ISLAMIC, BIBLICAL, AND WESTERN WORLDVIEWS

Category	Islamic	Biblical	Western[34]
God	Eternal, uncreated supreme deity considered merciful, wise and all powerful, though distant (deistic).	Eternal, uncreated supreme deity considered loving, just, merciful, wise and all-powerful, seeks relationship with humankind.	Does not exist.
Humankind	Created to serve Allah; believers dwell eternally in paradise, infidels returned to dust, unbelievers judged in hell.	Created and eternal image bearer of God, fallen due to sin but redeemable through faith in Christ.	Evolved mammal, socially defined morality, holds destiny in his own hands.

Category	Islamic	Biblical	Western[34]
Creation	Created by Allah to serve his purposes.	Created by God to display His glory and serve His purposes, will be restored to perfection.	Evolved and evolving.
Heaven/Hell	Eternal paradise largely appealing to masculine ideals, reserved for believers; eternal place of torment reserved for unbelievers.	Eternal paradise reserved for redeemed; eternal place of judgment reserved for unredeemed.	Do not exist.
Prayer	Prescribed ritual in which the believer acknowledges the greatness and uniqueness of Allah and makes requests but without assurance of response.	Communication for the purpose of praise, supplication, confession, or thanksgiving that God invites and to which He responds.	May have psychological benefits but not because of reality of a Divine Listener.
Angels/ Demons	Divine creatures serving as messengers, recorders, and guardians; fallen angels that tempt humankind to perform evil acts.	Divine creatures serving as God's messengers; fallen angels that tempt humankind to perform evil acts.	Do not exist.
Sin/Judgment	Forgetting or breaking the law of God for which ritual prayer and ablutions are prescribed. Allah stands as ultimate judge but mercy is granted based upon accumulated good works.	Violation of the law of God through commission or omission. God stands as holy Judge though forgiveness; salvation available through faith in Christ.	Moral boundaries are socially determined and judged. No moral absolutes, no final judgment.

Category	Islamic	Biblical	Western[34]
Time	Eternal and linear, moving toward the completion of God's plan.	Eternal and linear, moving toward the completion of God's plan.	Began with "Big Bang," linear and moving toward the extinction of life as we know it.

Figure 1 provides a visual representation of the relationship between the biblical, Western, and Muslim worldviews. The circles represent the values, beliefs, and practices that make up a given worldview. The overlap of any two circles represents beliefs, values, and practices that are commonly held between the two worldviews.[35] Likewise, the overlap of all three circles represents those things that all three hold in common.[36]

Figure 1
Worldview Overlap

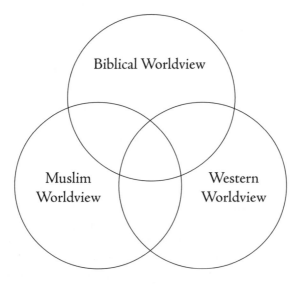

Though the circles representing the various worldviews are only conceptual in nature and are not intended to suggest the relative overlap of any one worldview with another, the image nevertheless does suggest that differences between the worldviews are real. The reality of these differences brings us to a question, "Is the apparent difference between the Western and biblical world-views a matter of intellectual sophistication or, rather, of progressive 'natural' revelation?" Does Western man's failure to fully accommodate the reality of the supernatural, and dreams and visions in particular, suggest that Western man's current sacred-secular dichotomy is neither entirely biblical nor valid? In this case would not those worldviews that still embrace such a view of the supernatural better approximate biblical Reality (with a capital "R")? In this regard, could not Western man learn from the Muslim worldview? As Morton Kelsey notes in his book, *God, Dreams and Revelation*, "It is harder for many modern-day Christians to experience God than it is for 'pagans' from other cultures. The modern church does not have a worldview that encourages serious belief in a spiritual reality."[37]

In his description of the historical development of the attitude toward dreams and visions in the church, Kelsey notes that every major father of the early church, from Justin Martyr to Origen to Cyprian, believed that dreams were a valid means of personal revelation.[38] He argues that for the "first 500-600 years of Christianity it was thought to be perfectly natural for a Christian to have a supernatural, spiritual encounter with Jesus. According to the theology of the day, such an encounter was the result of being filled with the Holy Spirit."[39] He continues his discussion by confirming that for the first 1,200 years of Christendom, dreams and visions were considered a viable means of knowing God and discerning His will. But Kelsey asks, "What brought an end to this tradition?"[40] His answer is revealing:

> ...in the thirteenth century, Thomas Aquinas tried to interpret the life of the church with the help of Aristotle's philosophy—the idea that man can experience (know) only through sensory perception and reason.[41]

As a result of Aquinas' influence, Western thought embarked upon an evolutionary trek that led to a secular-sacred dichotomy and a suspicion of the supernatural that is prevalent today.

Francis Schaeffer, in the first volume of his collected works, provides a helpful summary of this evolutionary trek that brought Western man to his current philosophical resting place. To illustrate this, Schaeffer poses a staircase image in which movement forward in history, and consequently "forward" in philosophical formulation, constitutes a downward movement and thus a departure from the biblical worldview. (See Figure 2.) As the figure illustrates, the first step down in the departure from biblical reality occurred in the realm of philosophy. As noted earlier, this downward movement is initiated in Aristotle, and in particular, in Thomas Aquinas' application of Aristotle's thought, which included "the insistence upon the independence of reason and philosophy from any constraint imposed by faith and theology."[42] Schaeffer's conclusion suggests that Aquinas' application of Aristotle led to a prevailing view in the West that man could acquire knowledge apart from revelation by using his own faculties of seeing, touching, smelling, tasting, hearing, and reasoning.

FIGURE 2
FRANCIS SHAEFFER'S VIEW OF THE PHILOSOPHICAL AND WORLDVIEW EVOLUTION OF THE WEST

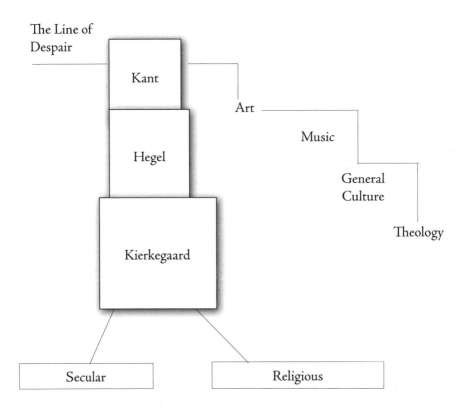

The departure from biblical reality is further precipitated by Aquinas' conclusion that although man's will was fallen, his intellect was not. Over time, this conclusion gave rise to the supposition that man's intellect, and ultimately man himself, was autonomous. Schaeffer continues his explanation of the influence of Aquinas' thought by noting that:

> The sphere of the autonomous growing out of Aquinas takes on various forms. One result, for example, was the development of natural theology. In this view, natural theology is a theology that could be pursued independently from the Scriptures.[43]

And thus natural theology and its conclusions are derived foremost from empirical evaluations and analytical exercises and not primarily from the Scriptures. Kelsey notes that the application of this thinking in the scientific realm led to the conclusion that humankind was bounded by a time-space box beyond which nothing exists. He asserts that if this conclusion is valid then "there is no possibility of dealing with the question of an irrational world,"[44] and therefore the supernatural is inaccessible.

As Schaeffer contends, the departure from biblical reality continued throughout history in the arenas of art, music, general culture, and finally, in theology. Initially, the introduction of Aristotelian thinking was limited to the educated and affluent, as they were the only ones with ready access to art, music, and literature. However, as the influence of this thinking moved into the realm of general culture affecting drama, recreation, and fashion, the humanistic philosophy of the specialists that was marked by the autonomy of humankind, came to roost in the hearts and minds of the layman and thus, began to be reflected in cultural shifts in behavior.

One of the results of the influence of Aquinas' philosophy was its effect on the way divine subjects were depicted in art. The adoption of Aquinas' philosophy served to cheapen previously upheld images and understandings of biblical reality while at the same time fostering an emphasis on nature, and in a roundabout way, on humankind himself. As Schaeffer continues to explain, the emerging focus on nature came at the expense of the previous focus (or at least obvious respect for the divine, what Schaeffer refers to as "grace"). Thus:

> …as nature was made autonomous, nature began to "eat up" grace. Through the Renaissance, from the time of Dante to Leonardo da Vinci, nature gradually became more and more autonomous. It was set free from God as the humanistic philosophers began to operate ever more freely. By the time the Renaissance reached its climax, nature had eaten up grace.[45]

Increasingly, Western culture reflected a humanistic emphasis, marked by relativistic values and a denial of absolutes, divorced from any universal truth.

According to Schaeffer, the final step in the departure from biblical reality occurred in theology. To understand how the application of Aristotelian philosophy affected theology, it is helpful to review the premises underlying the theology of Western man from the time of the Greeks forward. In short, Schaeffer denotes that in terms of theology, Western man was:

> *Rationalistic:* he begins absolutely and totally from himself, gathers information concerning the particulars, and formulates the universals, or absolutes.

> *Rational:* he acts on the basis that his aspiration concerning the validity of reason was well-founded. Men thought in terms of antithesis: "A" is not "non-A."

> Convinced that he would be able to construct a unified field of knowledge, and therefore: Rationalism + Rationality = a complete answer to all of thought and life.[46]

By the time of Kant (1724-1804) and Rousseau (1712-1778) however, rationalism was so fully entrenched that the concept of revelation no longer existed and "grace" (or the supernatural) no longer retained any meaning. In its place, the struggle was between nature and freedom. With the maturing of nature as autonomous, determinism emerged as a defining principle in contrast to an intense desire to exercise human freedom. The solution offered by Rousseau was to throw-off civilization and culture that hindered man's freedom and promote autonomous freedom of humankind—a freedom that has nothing to restrain it, which no longer fits into the rational world. It is freedom that "hopes and tries to will that the finite individual man will be free—and that which is left is individual self-expression."[47]

Changing the Rules

According to Schaeffer, the philosophical view that held to the ability of constructing a unified field of knowledge through rationalism and rationality prevailed until the time of Hegel (1770-1831). It was Hegel who concluded that a continued pursuit of a unified field of knowledge on the basis of antithesis was fruitless. Hegel proposed that instead, knowledge was the result of thesis giving way to antithesis with the answer being found in synthesis. In so stating, Schaeffer notes that Hegel changed the rules of the game in two areas: epistemology, the theory of knowledge and the limits of validity of knowledge; and methodology, the method by which we approach the question of truth and knowing. And thus he "changed the world," for now "all things are relativized."[48]

The fallout from Hegel resulted in what Schaeffer calls the "Line of Despair." This line separates what is reasonable from what is unreasonable. Initially, philosophy struggled with integrating nature and grace. By the time of Kant and Rousseau, that struggle was between nature and freedom. Under Hegel's influence the opponents of that struggle are faith and rationality. The resultant, inevitable despair of Hegel's philosophy emerges from the "abandonment of the hope of a unified answer for knowledge and life."

Following Hegel, the next significant contribution to the philosophic shift that led to the departure from biblical reality in theology was Soren Kierkegaard (1813-1855). It was Kierkegaard who proposed a means of re-connecting with the divine or "grace" (supernatural) but his proposition was rightly framed a "leap of faith" for it involved reaching into the non-rational to find hope. The philosophic conclusion prevalent in Kierkegaard's day was a dichotomy between faith and rationality in which all that remained on the side of rationality was mathematics, particulars, and mechanics. Man as man is dead; he has no meaning, no purpose, and no significance. Pessimism prevailed. On the side of faith was the supernatural, God, and optimism. But the only way to grab hold of this optimism was by a total non-rational, non-reasonable leap motivated by a non-rational faith.[49]

From Kierkegaard's system came the religious existentialism of Karl Barth. Under Barth's system, the Bible contains and transmits to us "a religious word" despite its perceived textual errors and contradictions. "Religious truth" is separated from historical truth and leaves no place for reason or historical verification. And thus, knowledge of God comes via non-rational experience or a religious leap.[50] Schaeffer goes on to say:

> Because the rational and logical are totally separated from the non-rational and the non-logical, the leap is total. Faith, whether expressed in secular or religious terms, becomes a leap without any verification because it is totally separated from the logical and reasonable.[51]

This brief summary of the departure from biblical reality on the part of Western man also describes the inevitable shift in his accompanying worldview. In sum, Western man has gradually discarded a worldview that considered the religious sphere of life, including its supernatural phenomena and its moral absolutes. In its place, he has adopted a view of life that is caught between, on the one hand, a mechanistic explanation of life, and on the other hand, a yearning for the divine. As a result, Western man is left with measuring the religious by the devices of his empiricism and satisfying his yearning for the divine through subjective, non-rational experience. This in turn has increasingly left the church unable to "speak" to modern man. As Kelsey notes:

> ...the Christian philosophies of the past three hundred years have overlooked the fact that God wants to come into contact with men and women and that they can actually know God. A division arose between the Church (who didn't want authority questioned) and the secular world because the Church refused to tolerate, let alone encourage, the part of scientific thought that allowed humans to discover that the earth revolves around the sun.

> The Church's intolerance of this inquiring spirit forced sci-
> entific thought to develop on a completely secular level and
> to become antireligious to the point of maintaining that
> human beings have no Godly spirit. This narrow-minded
> attitude eventually caused thinking Christians to adopt
> secular thought exclusively and become convinced that
> God could be known only through reason and not through
> experience. As a result of this type of thought, people came
> to believe that while God worked in World happenings,
> He could not be experienced personally.[52]

According to Schaeffer, the progression of thought in the West has led to a view that relegates supernatural phenomena to the non-rational and non-reliable. The difficulty for the Western Christian, however, lies in understanding and adopting the biblical worldview that clearly embraced such supernatural phenomena as dreams and visions, in contrast to his own worldview, which does not.

Before this chapter is concluded, it is of importance to note that there has been a relative rebound in the scientific community in the past 100 years with regard to the significance of the non-rational or supernatural, and of dreams in particular. Though it may have been thought that the influence of Aristotle would forever dominate the worldview of Western civilization, and that man would be left within the "time-space box with everything explained by his or her understanding of the 92 atoms, and the laws of Newton and Darwin,"[53] scientific discoveries in the late 19th and early 20th centuries increasingly suggested that the time-space box explanation was inadequate.

Of note was the discovery by Madame Curie near the turn of the 20th century that the 92 atoms (thought to be the elemental building blocks of matter, hence "elements") could be broken apart into innumerable pieces. With her discovery, the "known" became once more "unknown." Then, according to Kelsey:

> …one of the greatest modern mathematicians, Kurt Godel,
> ascertained that in mathematics discovery does not come

through sharp, well-developed reason, but through intuition.[54]

With this conclusion, the iron-clad logic of mathematics, one of the "hard" sciences of the mind, found itself affiliated with soul.

Then, it was none other than Teilhard de Chardin who argued that Darwin's system could not account for all the seemingly unwarranted or untimely mutations and jumps that frequently occur. And again, scientific theory, which yearned to account for all the evidence, found itself held up to the light of inquiry that exposed its weaknesses and limitations.

Finally, Kelsey notes that a final area of modern science that challenges the adequacy of the time-space box theory is psychomatic medicine. Here he records how through a series of studies, modern doctors have identified a correlation between personal health and the relationship of a person to his or her spiritual and physical environment. He further comments that even Carl Jung admits to a spiritual reality that provides a benefit to certain patients. Kelsey states that Jung, "…had never seen a case of neurosis that was actually cured until the neurotic person was brought in touch with that reality of which all living religions speak."[55]

As a result of the discoveries noted above (and many others too numerous to mention) the prevailing opinion as expressed by Aristotle and applied by Aquinas, that true knowledge is gained only through reason and experience, was significantly eroded, pushing humankind once again to look beyond the rational for answers. Probably nowhere has this search beyond the rational gone further than in the arena of psychology. And as a result, dreams have once again emerged as sources or means of knowledge, and of possible vehicles of divine communication.

The modern individual most responsible for bringing dreams back into the mainstream of the Western worldview is Sigmund Freud. His book, *The Interpretation of Dreams* (first published in 1913), was a summary of his study and findings relative to the phenomena of dreams in individuals under his medical care (including himself). In his book, Freud sets out to demonstrate that the interpretation of dreams was in fact a key to the treatment of neuroses and psychoses. Though Freud was convinced that dreams were simply a product of the psyche, albeit a sometimes complex one, he expressed his opinion of the value of study of such by noting:

> I should expect to find the theoretical value of the study of dreams in its contribution to psychological knowledge and in its preparation for an understanding of neuroses. Who can foresee the importance of a thorough knowledge of the structure and activities of the psychic apparatus when even our present state of knowledge produces a happy therapeutic influence in the curable forms of psychoneurosis? What about the practical value of such study someone may ask? (Is it only) for psychic knowledge and for the discovering of the secret peculiarities of individual character? Have not the unconscious feelings revealed by the dream the value of real forces in the psychic life? Should we take lightly the ethical significance of the suppressed wishes which, as they now create dreams, may some day create other things?[56]

For Freud, dreams were purely a psychological phenomenon, the outward manifestation of an internalized conflict. In Freud's terms, a dream was an expression of the fulfillment of a wish. Thus, the particulars of a dream and its subsequent meaning were related to conscious or unconscious (and often repressed) desires. He argued that:

> …the more one is occupied with the solution of dreams, the more willing one must become to acknowledge that the majority of dreams of adults treat of sexual material and give expression to erotic wishes…let us recognize at once that this fact is not to be wondered at, but that it is in complete harmony with the fundamental assumption of dream explanation. No other impulse has had to undergo so much suppression from the time of childhood as the sex impulse in its numerous components, from no other impulse have survived so many and such intense unconscious wishes, which now act in the sleeping state in such a manner as to produce dreams.[57]

Freud further concluded that although dreams originated from within and looked back to previous event(s), their value was not only confined to retrospection. He stated:

> And how about the value of the dream for a knowledge of the future? That, of course, we cannot consider. One feels inclined to substitute, 'for a knowledge of the past.' For the dream originates from the past in every sense. To be sure the ancient belief that the dream reveals the future is not entirely devoid of truth. By representing to us a wish as fulfilled the dream certainly leads us to the future; but this future, taken by the dreamer as present, has been formed into the likeness of that past by the indestructible wish.[58]

Freud noted that though the experiences of the most recent day are found in every dream, the sources of a dream may include any of the following:

> a) a recent and psychologically significant experience that is directly represented in the dream.
>
> b) several recent, significant experiences, which are united by the dream into a whole.
>
> c) one or more recent and significant experiences, which are represented in the dream by the mention of a contemporary but indifferent experience.
>
> d) a subjective significant experience (a recollection, train of thought), which is regularly represented in the dream by the mention of a recent but indifferent impression.[59]

In the analysis of a dream, Freud would probe the elements, events, and persons to try to identify the underlying plot or conflict. Functioning from within his own worldview, which suggested that humankind lived within a time-space box, Freud pressed to find a rational, patient-defined explanation for the dream itself. Because his worldview did not allow for outside, personal influence, dreams were, for Freud, simply coded episodes depicting personal compulsions. Thus he concluded that dreams served as signposts for often unconscious desires that played themselves out as the fulfillment of a wish.

The fact that Freud's analysis of the meaning and purpose of dreams survived has resulted in a reintroduction of the integrity of dreams and dreaming to the West. That he did so from the perspective of medicine, even psychology, has given dreams a societal respectability that has grown with the improved perception of psychology. However, Freud was unwilling in his analysis of dreams to allow for origins outside of his subject's previous experiences.

Within 50 years of Freud's book, another prominent psychologist, Carl Jung, introduced an adjustment to the meaning and purpose of dreams as defined earlier by Freud.[60] Jung disagreed with Freud that dreams were "a mere facade, behind which something has been carefully hidden."[61] Dreams, according to Jung, are nothing more than what they appear to be. Jung said:

> ...the dream is such a difficult and intricate subject, that I do not dare to make any assumptions about its possible cunning. The dream is a natural event and there is no reason under the sun why we should assume that it is a crafty device to lead us astray.[62]

For Jung dream analysis and interpretation involved identifying the major elements, events, and people of a dream or dreams and assigning self-evident meaning to them. Because Jung understood dreams as links in a series of conscious-unconscious events, he felt justified in establishing symbolic meaning to recurring or common dream elements. He stated:

> As there is a continuity in consciousness, despite the fact that it is regularly interrupted by sleep, there is probably also a continuity of unconscious processes and perhaps even more so than with the events of consciousness. In any case my experience is in favor of the probability that dreams are the visible links in a chain of unconscious events.[63]

Probably Jung's most significant departure from Freud is his allowance for the Divine Person as a source for dreams and their elements. In defining his worldview that accommodates an outside influence in the psychology of humankind, Jung first traces the historical decline of supernaturalism in the West. Jung notes:

> Since those days [of the Reformation] Protestantism has become a hotbed of schisms and, at the same time, of a rapid increase of science and technics which attracted human consciousness to such an extent that it forgot the unaccountable forces of the unconscious mind.[64]

Jung continued by noting that such a shift in religious opinion had a significant dampening effect on the religious perception of those who made up the church. He observed that:

> ...to ancient man the dream was sent by God, and while the Church still allows this possibility (only very cautiously, and reserving to itself the right to adjudicate in the matter), popular opinion today has deprecated this kind of psychic activity to such an extent that it is often believed that dreams are merely the result of physical causes, such as sleeping in an uncomfortable position, or eating a heavy meal before going to bed.[65]

Jung notes that the departure from acceptance of the divine in dreams was strangely enough nurtured by the church itself in an attempt to maintain orthodoxy. He states:

> There are any amount of creeds and ceremonies that exist for the sole purpose of forming a defense against the unexpected, dangerous tendencies of the unconscious. The peculiar fact that the dream is the divine voice and messenger and yet an unending source of trouble, does not disturb the primitive mind. We still find obvious remnants of this primitive fact in the psychology of the Jewish prophets. Often enough they hesitate to listen to the voice. ...Since the dawn of mankind there has been a marked tendency to delimit the unruly and arbitrary "supernatural" influence by definite forms and laws. And this process has gone on in history by the multiplication of rites, institutions and

creeds. In the past two thousand years we find the institution of the Christian Church assuming a mediating and protective function between these influences and man. It is not denied in medieval ecclesiastical writings that a divine influx could take place in dreams, for instance, but this view is not exactly encouraged and the Church reserves the right to decide whether a revelation is to be considered authentic or not. In spite of the fact that the Church recognizes the undeniable emanation of certain dreams from God, it is disinclined, even positively averse, to any serious occupation with dreams, while admitting that some might contain an immediate revelation. Thus the change in mental attitudes which has taken place in recent centuries is from this point of view at least, not wholly unwelcome to the Church because it has effectively discouraged the former introspective attitude which was favorable to a serious consideration of dreams and inner experiences.[66]

In bemoaning this neglect of the non-rational, Jung argues that simply to deny the possibility of outside influences does not negate their reality. Again Jung notes that:

If we take into consideration the fact that God is an "unscientific" hypothesis, we can easily explain why people have forgotten to think along such lines. And even if they cherish a certain belief in God they would be deterred from the idea of God within by their religious education, which always depreciated this idea as "mystical." Yet it is precisely this "mystical" idea which is enforced by the natural tendencies of the unconscious mind.[67]

And so, Jung upholds the possibility that some dreams have an outside source both in their content as well as in their occurrence, which may in many instances be divine. In so doing he aligns himself with the prevailing opinion of the early church fathers that dreams were a means of divine encounter. And though he considers himself incompetent to correctly apply the metaphysical and philosophical considerations and implications of his observations,[68] he clearly acknowledges that there is more to dreams and their interpretations than a collective consideration of internal conflict.

COMMUNICATING THE GOSPEL TO MUSLIMS

What does all this have to do with evangelism in a Muslim context? Simply put, the Christian, and in particular the Western Christian, whose aim is to communicate the gospel to Muslims, must understand both the Muslim's worldview and that of his own. The Western Christian must realize that in one sense the Muslim, to the extent that he has escaped Aristotelian influence (that reality can only be known through sensory perception and reason), will be more receptive to experiential phenomena—such as dreams and visions—than he is. The Western Christian must then consider the fact that effective communication to this Muslim must somehow take into consideration the role of experiential phenomena.

In communicating the gospel to the Muslim, however, the Christian is not operating from within a vacuum. The Scriptures provide both the content of the gospel (see 1 Cor. 15:1-4) as well as the parameters that define the limits of gospel communication and appropriate behavior of the gospel witness.

In short, he is to follow the example of Christ in his living (see Eph. 5:1) and the example of Paul in his preaching (see 1 Cor. 11:1; Phil. 3:17; 2 Thess. 3:7,9). And in so doing, the Christian is free to utilize all that the Scripture authorizes in an effort to effectively communicate. It is therefore imperative that he make an effort to understand the respective worldviews from which he comes and into which he goes so as to identify where each of these overlap with the biblical worldview. It is then to his advantage, with regard to maximizing the potency of his communication, that he utilize that overlap as an avenue of communication for the gospel.

In terms of dreams and visions, the Christian must realize that all dreams are not revelatory neither obviously nor potentially so. Surely some, perhaps even the majority, are simply the products of normal physiological functions as noted by Freud and Jung. However, the historical, experiential, and philosophical data suggest that the physiological mechanics of dreams are available for divine use, and in the worldview of the Muslim, such may be the means used of God to effectively prepare an individual to "hear" the gospel message and motivate him or her to respond to it.

๑๏ๆ๏ๆ๏ๆ

POINTS TO PONDER

1. How would you describe Muslim receptivity to dream and vision experiences?

2. To what do you attribute the level of receptivity and responsiveness that Muslims have with regard to dreams and visions?

3. How does formal Islam differ from folk or popular Islam? How much effect does popular Islam have on the average Muslim today?

4. What happened in the history of Western civilization that affected how Westerners view and respond to the supernatural, of which dreams and visions are a part?

5. To what can you attribute the change on the part of some in the West with regard to their receptivity and responsiveness to the supernatural, including dreams and visions?

CHAPTER 6

Dreams and Visions and Muslim Conversions

Surely conversion is a matter between man and his Maker who alone knows His creatures' hearts. —Mohandas Gandi

I revealed myself to those who did not ask for me; I was found by those who did not seek me. To a nation that did not call on my name, I said, "Here am I, here am I." —Isaiah 65:1 NIV

The phenomenon of Muslim conversion to Christianity as a result of dreams and visions is well-documented. That God uses dreams and visions to draw Muslim men and women to Himself from all walks of life is no longer hidden in long-lost personal diaries. Moving, firsthand accounts dating from the Medieval Period through to the present day can be found in mission histories, in biographies, in magazine articles, in television and radio interviews, and in a recent DVD release, *More than Dreams*.[1] And yet, despite the widespread popularity and availability of such stories, what is lacking in many of these articles and media presentations is a discussion of the implications for Christian witness.

So what can we learn about how God uses dreams and visions in Muslim conversion? Does the fact that Muslims live in a worldview in which dream and vision experiences are understood to be divine channels make a difference in how we talk to our Muslim friend about what he or she experiences? Are all dream and vision experiences the same? Do the circumstances of the life of the dreamer make a difference? What happens once the dream and vision is experienced? Does the dreamer automatically understand the symbolism and imagery?

In an effort to uncover answers to these and other similar questions we need to take a look at a number of personal accounts of dream and vision experiences. After reviewing these stories, the important features will be identified. These recurring features and the responses they provoke in the life of the dreamer will in turn suggest how God is using these supernatural experiences to bring about conversion from Islam to Christianity. Finally, once the pattern or patterns of divine cause and effect are noted, their implications for Christian witness among Muslims can be discussed.

In addition to the individual biographical and historical accounts of Muslim conversion that can be found, one singularly important resource are the commentaries of Constance Padwick[2] on the journals of Lilias Trotter, missionary to Algeria[3] in the late 19th and early 20th centuries. Padwick's carefully documented and organized treatment of the personal stories that she gleaned from these diaries provide a significant look into the world of the supernatural that resulted in conversion for many Muslims, both men and women.

Padwick begins her discussion by reviewing and categorizing the dream and vision events that are recorded in the Bible under four general categories:

1. **Moral Warning**—example: Pilate's Wife (Matt. 27:19)

2. **Guidance**—example: Joseph/Mary's departure into Egypt (Matt. 2:13)

3. **Encouragement**—example: God's Encouragement of Paul during the shipwreck (Acts 27:24) and

4. **The Presence (of God/Christ)**—example: Stephen's stoning (Acts 7:56)

She then goes on to retell and comment on those stories that fall into each of the above categories and that illustrate how they were instrumental in bringing the Muslim dreamer to the brink of conversion.[4] What is clear from the stories of the people concerned by the dream and vision event is that the breadth of circumstances, the range of personal issues, and the differences in the dream or vision experiences which God utilizes to motivate individuals to seek Him are practically limitless. A review of the anecdotal evidence taken from Padwick's gleanings from the Lilias Trotter diaries and other extemporaneous sources follows.

Moral Warning as an Avenue to Christ

Dream or vision events that convey a moral warning do so by presenting a threat of judgment and an option or appeal to escape such judgment. In a fashion similar to Saul's encounter on the Damascus road, this dream or vision type often delivers a stirring reproach to an individual that, due the drama of impending doom that it conveys, often gives rise to a remarkable transformation (cf. Saul, Acts 27:2-23). As an example of this dream or vision type Padwick retells this account:

> An old man tottering with age (who came to visit the missionary) said: "I had an awful dream last night, which today has haunted me with misery. The Most High said to me: 'O Sheikh, you are near the gates of Heaven, but because of your sins you cannot enter in.' God has now sent you (the missionary) to me to tell me the way of hope. When I get home I shall go to a secret place I know of and say: "O God, I have sinned against Thee. I shall return like the wayward boy in your parable."[5]

In this instance an aged man, who according to Padwick's source had no prior Christian teaching, was confronted both with the brevity of his remaining life and the barrier between him and Heaven—his sin. Despite his life-long commitment to Islam and its associated beliefs that would normally have prompted him to appeal to the mercy of Allah, this man felt compelled to seek out the resident missionary to inquire of "the way of hope" so he could "return like the wayward boy in your parable"—an obvious reference to the story of the Prodigal Son found in Luke 15.

In another example of a moral warning dream or vision event, Padwick recounts this:

Blind Houriya came this morning with "I want to tell you something that has frightened me very much. I dreamt it Saturday night, but I was too frightened to tell you yesterday. Today my husband told me, "You must tell them." I dreamed that a great snake was twisting (a)round my throat and strangling me. I called to you but you said: "I cannot save you, for you are not following our road." I went on calling for help, and one came up to me and loosened the snake from off my neck. I said: "And who is it that is saving me, and what is this snake?" A voice said: "I am Jesus and this snake is Ramadan."[6]

Here the judgment and consequent option or appeal to escape is couched in the image of the coiling snake. That the woman fully understood the implications of the image is evidenced in her willingness to bring this to the attention of her husband and to break her fast (which the extended account describes). Again the resolution to the conflict raised by this dream or vision encounter is found in the interaction with the resident missionary who is able to explain to the woman how to follow the right road.

A third example of this dream or vision type is again noted by Padwick:

Up ran Mustapha with a shining face. Jesus had come to him in a dream and had shown him two doors—the door of Heaven and the door of Hell—and asked him which he would like to enter. I said: "The door of Heaven," and He said: "I must wash you before you can enter that door." And I said: "Lord, wash me," and I woke. In his simple boy way he knelt and gave his heart up to the Lord.[7]

According to the diary entry of Lilias Trotter, Mustapha had been attending classes on the Christian faith at the mission house and thus had had some exposure to Christian material prior to the dream or vision event. In this case, the judgment and option or appeal motif is evident in the image of the two doors. Somehow the boy clearly understood that a failure to be washed meant that the door to Heaven would forever remain closed. The extended account of this incident tells how the boy was led to understand the assurance of having his sins washed away by Jesus upon visiting the resident missionary.

These examples of what Padwick classifies as "moral warning" demonstrate that the threat of judgment found in this type of dream or vision event provides a very significant motivation to the dreamer to consider Christianity. Somehow, the dreamer clearly understands that he or she is faced with a choice that carries ultimate consequences. Interestingly, despite the force of the moral warning, the dream or vision event does not rule out the necessary participation of a Christian friend or neighbor (or even the local missionary or pastor) whose role is to put the dreamer's dream and response to it into the context of the gospel. Such as in the following story:

> One of the first (Muslims to respond) was a strange woman who arrived at the door (of Lilias Trotter) and asked to come in. "I dreamed a dream," she said, "A man came to me in a white robe and told me to go and hear about Sidna Aissa (the Muslim name for Jesus). Three times he said it and I asked, 'Where shall I go?' The man told me to come to this house, so I hung out my laundry and came with great joy."[8]

GUIDANCE AS AN AVENUE TO CHRIST

Dreams and visions that primarily provide guidance successfully communicate directives and make use of symbolic images designed to lead the dreamer into further inquiry of Christ, the Christian faith, or other ultimate issues. In contrast to the moral warning dream or vision type, the guidance dream does not generally employ fierce dramatic images designed to compel an individual to make a change or face ultimate consequences.

However, the message of the guidance dream or vision experience helps the dreamer who may be still on the fence with regard to his or her faith, come to a clear understanding of which path to take.

As an example of the guidance dream or vision type, Padwick includes this story:

> Today the storm had blown over and her face was quiet and bright as she bent over the bit of gargaff (handicraft) I had

brought her to pass the time. Then she let the work drop and began to talk: "I have had a dream," she said. "It was the night after you were here. I saw two kanouns (fire pots). In one was a very little fire, nearly going out; in the other was a bright fire that was increasing. Someone was standing by and he said: 'Knowest thou what these two fires mean?' I said: 'No.' He went on: 'The little fire that is nearly out is the religion of the Arabs. They pray and give alms and witness and fast, and they say *inshallah* we shall go to Heaven. But the bright fire is what your friend has told you about Jesus. There is certainty about that. You have to leave the old fire and come to the new.' 'I believed before,' she said, 'I believed but now I know…I am one of you now and the sister of the others in the world.'"[9]

In this incident, the encouragement to seek out the Christian faith is found both in the words of the dream messenger, "You have to leave the old fire and come to the new." Furthermore, the image of the firepots helped the dreamer to clarify exactly what was in the past versus what was in the future. In effect, the message communicated by the dream was, "do you want to die out with the flame in the first fire pot (the old way, Islam), or burn free and strong with the new one (the new way, with Jesus)?" The motivation to follow through is enabled by the reference to the missionary friend as well as by the comment by the dream messenger that in Christianity there is certainty. The success of the dream event is accounted for by the dreamer's admission that "I am one of you now."

A final example of this dream or vision type recorded by Padwick says:

Zuleikha went away yesterday, gloomy and huffy, as is often the case when her soul is wrong. Today she is back again with her face soft and shining. "Yes, I have come to tell you. In the night I dreamt that someone came to me and said: 'One who is your father is downstairs and wants you.' I answered: 'My father is dead.' But I went down to see. A man stood there and said to me: 'Come with me and see your sister,' I said: 'My sister lives far away in El Kantara (a suburb of the town).' 'No matter,' He answered; 'come and see her.' So I followed Him and He brought me to this house and led me up to this room and called you in and said: 'This is your sister.' Then I turned to Him and kissed His shoulder (a sign of reverence), and He looked into my face and held up His hand and said: 'Follow Me and fear not. Follow Me and fear not.' And I awoke. I told my Maula (the owner of the house) that I must keep His road and break Ramadan again, and I went and told Taitum and now I have come to the house of my sister. Give me a bit of bread that I may eat it before you (to show you that I am breaking the fast of Ramadan, and hence I am now a follower of Jesus)."[10]

Here the guidance motif is ultimately indicated at the end of the dream by the invitation to the dreamer to follow Him, that is, Jesus Christ. The initial motivation to follow is provided by the invitation to the dreamer to see her father, and later, to visit her sister. Though the result of the visit-her-sister episode in the dream differed from her natural inclination (that she would visit her biological sister who lived far away), the woman immediately understood the significance of the meeting when the lady she met turned out not to be her sister, but the resident missionary. It was this dream encounter that ultimately motivated the dreamer to turn from Islam, evidenced in her breaking the fast of Ramadan, and turning to Christ.

The guidance dream or vision type is somewhat less direct than the moral warning dream/vision as a means of influence in motivating an individual to follow Christ. Certainly this type of dream may provide that kind of guidance, and the dream events cited demonstrate that. However, the purpose of this dream or vision type is broader and may find an application in a range of other issues such as relationships, business, or in providing assistance in making personal decisions.

For those incidents not directly concerned with gospel issues, the role of the Christian friend as an interpreter of the information portrayed by the dream or vision may be less critical. That is to say that it may be possible that the dreamers could understand all that they need to in order to receive the full benefit of the dream or vision event without help from a Christian friend. However, the evidence suggests otherwise.

In reality, the full benefit from the experience hinges on discovering the connection of the message of the dream or vision experience to the life situation of the dreamer with the help of the Christian friend. When the dreamer is wrestling both with the reality that he or she is struggling (with life issues) and confronted with Truth that perhaps contradicts personal beliefs, the person not only needs to be shown the way, but also to have the struggle acknowledged, confirmed, and put into perspective that he or she can grasp. It really is all about connecting, and for this, the wise counsel of a Christian friend is indispensable to hold up the light of Truth so as to help the dreamer find and follow the right path.

Encouragement as an Avenue to Christ

A third dream or vision type described by Padwick is identified by the positive emotional benefit it provides. Dreams and visions sent to encourage the dreamers tend to occur amidst difficult circumstances, whether physical or emotional in nature. In these instances, an encounter with Christ or a prescribed path to "follow" (typical of the moral warning and guidance dream or vision types respectively) is replaced by an image or announcement of divine favor providing assurance and confirmation that leads to encouragement. One such story, told by Padwick, follows:

> (Ahmad) the Younger had a dream that has laid fresh hold on him. The Lord came to him and said: "Thou hast been much in darkness. I will take it away." And He passed His hand over (Ahmad's) eyes and wiped the darkness out, and then drew with His finger an arch on his forehead, which meant a rainbow with its promise that the clouds would not prevail. "Go forward and fear not to eat," He said (it was Ramadan), and both (Ahmad) and his wife have broken the fast in their room.[11]

Typical of the encouragement type dream or vision, a prominent symbol or image (in this case, a rainbow) is given. The purpose of the image is to prolong the sense of the encouragement by serving as an aid to memory of the event. What is lacking in this dream or vision type is any reference to an encounter with Christ, a threat of judgment, or a directive to go a certain way or to perform a certain act. What is evident is an announcement of divine favor regarding current behavior or a recent or future decision to be made by the dreamer (in this case, whether to break the fast of Ramadan).

Another example from Padwick states:

> I asked Aisha, the muezzin's wife, how long it was since the light had come. The predominating point seemed to be a dream of a few weeks ago. She was standing among a crowd near the gates of Heaven, wondering if she could get in, and the Lord Jesus came out and took her hand under the wing of His burnous and led her in. 'Since then all has been full of joy,' she said, 'and His words have been as a field full of flowers.' I can quite believe that this would be a great seal to her faith, for a lurking terror among Muslim converts [to Christianity] is that they will belong to nobody at the last.[12]

Here again what is dominant in this dream event is an image that serves to provide confirmation to the dreamer that he or she has made the right choice and is following the right path. In this case the image is that of Jesus taking Aisha's hand and leading her into Heaven. As the commentary to the dream provided by the resident missionary notes, this image of belonging to someone at the end of life, served as a profound source of confidence, assurance, and encouragement that God would show ultimate favor to her.

A third example provided by Padwick tells this story:

> Fatima over the way told us today that last night she went up to sleep very heavy because one of the women had been calling her a metournia (renegade). "I dreamed, and Jesus was there—just as He was in the picture you showed us on Saturday. He said to me: 'I am always here, Fatima, and I always hear you call to me, but you do not call very often. And I know you are troubled about Kheira; you are afraid she will get into harm when you are out.' (Kheira is her

wild fifteen-year-old sister, left on her hands as a tiny child by her dying mother.) 'I will keep Kheira,' and He laid His hands on Kheira's shoulder, 'I am always here.' And her face shone as she told it."[13]

This dream event displays the classic features of the encouragement dream or vision type. The woman's personal and family situation has put her in need of help. The message in the dream was one of confirmation that God was present and active. The dream event that comes to her is built around the expression of divine favor (in this case in conversation as opposed to a significant image), which speaks directly to her circumstances.

Similar to the guidance dream or vision type, the encouragement dream or vision type may address a number of personal issues that extend beyond gospel questions. The apparent purpose of the encouragement dream or vision is to grant the dreamer a sense of divine approval confirming their faith and God's presence in their circumstances, no matter how difficult, which in turn gives a sense of confidence, assurance, and encouragement. Here again, the role of a Christian friend is indispensable as they serve as an instrument of God to help connect the message of the dream or vision to the life circumstances of the dreamer.

The Presence as an Avenue to Christ

What distinguishes the last category of dream or vision events described by Padwick is the dominant image of the person of Jesus Christ. In dreams of this type little, if anything, is reported as being said by Jesus or those who appear with Him. Instead, the impact of seeing the divine figure is all that is needed to convey the intended message.

From the stories included in her writings, apparently most of the dreams and visions of this type occur as the dreamers approach death. However, near-death circumstances are not necessarily essential to prepare the dreamer for this type of encounter. Of note are the following death-bed dream events that Padwick includes:

> Poor old Aisha has had a dream, the first sign of any spontaneous movement in the dark soul. She tried to tell

it feebly to H. yesterday. It was Jesus standing before her, not with the white garments that most of them see, but with the Precious Blood flowing down. Today she is hardly conscious. Was it the last chance that God took for reaching her before the clouds of the dark valley closed in?[14]

And again:

The new Fatima is a touching soul. She is very, very ill, unable to lie down now, night or day. She sits when we go to see her, with her arms resting on a stool and her head upon them. But when we speak of Jesus she rouses out of semi-stupor. "Yes, He washed my heart like this," and she passes her hand over it…."And He is here in this room…the others cannot see Him, but I see Him;" and the poor face lights up. "He comes and speaks to me, and I ask Him when He will come for me. He was standing over there, in that corner by the window, last night…. No, they cannot see Him…I can see Him…." And the breath fails and her head sinks down again.[15]

These two stories reveal the typical content of the presence dream or vision type. In contrast to the others, the scope and content of its subject matter is limited to the presence of the person of Jesus.

Additionally, Jesus is generally not noted as speaking or performing any sort of personally significant act. Rather, the message of the dream/vision is simply conveyed by the "picture" of Jesus in the dream. It is notable that Jesus' appearance as portrayed in the various accounts varies from story to story. Apparently the message Jesus is intending to convey is directly related to the particular way in which He presents Himself in a particular dream.

For instance, in Aisha's dream in which Jesus is presented with blood flowing from wounds—the image of the crucified and resurrected Savior—brought her comfort and assurance that Heaven awaited, forgiveness was hers, and that her faith had been acknowledged and confirmed. For Fatima, Jesus comes as a visiting friend. His recurring visits to stand and speak with her as she fades from life to death serve to relieve whatever anxiety she may have about death and dying and confirm her faith.

As in the moral warning dream or vision type, the presence dream or vision type deals almost exclusively with ultimate spiritual issues, and the dreamer is faced with responding to the message that the dream or vision conveys by the particular image of Jesus presented. It is surmised, though the dream or vision events recorded by Padwick do not include such detail, that the participation of a Christian friend would again be essential in assisting the dreamer in understanding the message of the dream or vision in light of the gospel. Furthermore, the Christian friend, in hearing the dream or vision story, shares in the rejoicing of the comfort and confirmation received and then is privileged to relay the scene to others.

The dream or vision events described here are but a small sample of the everyday occurrences of dream or vision phenomena that I believe the Lord is utilizing to motivate Muslims to turn to and follow Christ. A careful analysis of these stories leads to the following conclusions:

1. God can and does use previously acquired information about Himself, despite the fact that sometimes the information is woefully incomplete, to draw people to Himself through supernatural means, such as dreams and visions.

   What is interesting to note is that sometimes incidental contact with Christian content is all that is necessary. Take the example of Fatima. Her dream was based upon a picture of Jesus she had seen a few days prior to the actual dream event. Furthermore, the images, symbols, and other beings—whether Jesus or angels—who appear in the dreams, fit the Muslim perception of what they should look like. So Jesus is often seen dressed in a white robe; the attire of a religious man in Islam. This is the case in the dream of the unknown woman who came to the home of Lilias Trotter at the request of the white-robed man.

2. These dreams and visions apparently come unannounced, unprovoked, or induced and the dreamer is often left with a sense of urgency to respond but uncertain how to do so.

   Muslim scholar Ibn Khaldun admits that though the capacity to experience dreams is given to all, the occurrence of dreams and visions and the content of them occurs "unintentionally without their (the person) having power over it. The soul occupies itself with a thing. As a result, it obtains that glimpse (of the supernatural) while it is asleep, and it sees that thing. (But) it does not plan it that way."[16]

For some, difficult life circumstances provide fertile ground for God to intervene with a word of warning or direction. For others, the approach of death due to extended illness or advanced age set the stage for an invitation to turn to Jesus.

Despite the apparent effectiveness that dreams and visions have in motivating the dreamer to respond positively to Jesus and the Christian faith, it is apparently left up to God and His intent to communicate with a given person that determines if and when they will have such an experience, and what will be its content. As will be shown in a later chapter, nowhere does the Bible give instruction or any indication that dreams and visions can be induced or result from personal effort.

3. The role of a Christian friend is crucial as a link to assisting the dreamer in understanding and responding appropriately to the message received.

In each instance in which the dreamer is faced with the urgency to respond to ultimate spiritual issues, the choice is monumental. Leaving the Muslim faith and embracing the Christian faith is a choice that comes with a high cost. A Muslim convert to Christianity is considered a traitor and an apostate. He or she may lose his or her job or education, be rejected by his or her family and friends, or even lose his or her life depending on the context. The Christian friend in these cases plays not only the role of interpreter to help the dreamer understand the message of the dream or vision and recognize the right path to follow, but also that of comforter and personal assistant as the reality and consequences of the person's conversion takes shape. Such is the role that Ananias played for Saul during the tumultuous time following his conversion (see Acts 9:10-19).

With the stakes so high, especially for the dreamer, the real question becomes one of discerning truth. Because dreams and visions sometimes convey a message that calls for radical change or that makes use of images and symbols that require interpretation, understanding the message and knowing how to respond is crucial. If obeying the words of a person dressed in white could cause someone to be disowned by his family or cost him his life, he better be sure that he knows what is real and what is worth listening to. But this issue of discerning truth brings us to the next set of questions. Because dreams and visions are somewhat rare as are other-worldly experiences, how can one know what is true and should be accepted and what is false and should be rejected? How can one be sure that choosing the path indicated in the dream or vision experience is the right one?

Discerning the Truth

The use of anecdotal evidence such as the stories you've read in this book raises the issue of the relationship between personal experience and truth. Clearly our own experience tells us that there are all sorts of dream and vision experiences that have nothing at all to do with ultimate spiritual questions. In some instances, the dream contains nothing more than a strange mix of unrelated people engaged in unrelated events in unrelated places that stir up worry, fear, and wonder or simply leaves us scratching our heads.

But for those dreams and visions that clearly intend to communicate a spiritual message, the questions remain: What is the relationship of the dream or vision experience to what is real and what is true? How does the message of a particular dream or vision relate to the message of the Bible? Just because someone thinks that God spoke to him in a dream or vision, does that necessarily make the dream or vision worth listening to? How should a dream or vision event be regarded if it provides information or directs the dreamer to believe or act in a matter that is contrary to the things that Jesus taught and stood for?

In short, what are the criteria for judging the validity of dreams and visions that truly originate with the God of the Bible; and hence should be heeded? And how can one discern if a given dream or vision experience originates from somewhere or someone else and should be ignored?

The Old Testament law that God gave to Israel through Moses sheds some light on the criteria for judging the validity of dreams and visions. Deuteronomy 13:1-5a says:

> *If a prophet or dreamer of dreams arises among you and gives a sign or a wonder, and the sign or the wonder comes true, concerning which he spoke to you, saying, 'Let us go after other gods (whom you have not known) and let us serve them,' you shall not listen to the words of that prophet or that dreamer of dreams;...You shall follow the Lord your God and fear Him; and you shall keep His commandments, listen to His voice, serve Him, and cling to Him. But that prophet or dreamer of dreams shall be put to death, because he has counseled rebellion against the Lord your God...*

What is clear from this text is that the validation of a prophet or dreamer of dreams was to be found in his orientation toward the Lord. If the prophet or dreamer of dreams counseled people to follow the Lord and keep His commandments, his words could be trusted because his message would be seen to have the stamp of divine origin. If, however, he counseled people to follow after other gods, even if the sign or wonder of which he spoke came to pass, he and his message were to be rejected because it did not conform to the recorded directives of the Lord.

The apostle Paul alludes to a similar means of validating the message and messenger of the Gospel in his letter to the Galatians. In Galatians 1:8, Paul says, "*But even if we, or an angel from heaven* [reference to a visionary experience], *should preach to you a gospel contrary to what we have preached to you, he is to be accursed!*"

Here, as in Deuteronomy, the test of the validity of the message was its orientation to the Lord, and His previously recorded teaching. So the litmus test for truthfulness of a given dream or vision experience is the whole of God's revealed truth contained in the Bible. And in the particular case in which the dreamer is confronted with a choice with regard to the Christian faith, the criteria that must be used to judge the message is the biblical content of the gospel: Does the dream and vision point the subject toward Christ as the only Savior? Is the means of salvation presented in the dream or vision in agreement with the Scriptures?

Does the message present a picture of God, man, and man's spiritual condition that lines up with that shown in the Bible? If so, then it passes the test defined by both Old and New Testaments. If not, then the message must be rejected and the dream and vision experience must be understood as having a non-heavenly origin.

But is that all that there is to it? Does the Bible have anything else to say about dreams and visions? Are there examples of God sending dreams and visions to any of His people that could serve as an example as to how He intended them to be understood and heeded? Were people warned or guided by dreams or visions? Was anyone encouraged or helped by the presence of Christ in a dream or vision event? Does the Bible record incidents in which dreams and visions were instrumental in conversion?

◦▼◦▼◦▼◦

POINTS TO PONDER

1. How does the moral warning dream or vision experience contribute to conversion for a Muslim?

2. Both the guidance and the encouragement dream or vision types make use of significant images or symbols to convey their message. What purpose do these images and symbols have for the dreamer?

3. In the presence dream or vision type, the divine figure rarely speaks and yet the dreamer recognizes the divine figure as God. How does the dreamer make this connection?

4. Dreams and visions that lead to conversion apparently draw from or build upon exposure to Christian information to which the dreamer has had exposure. What does this suggest about the importance of sharing Christian literature, DVDs, Bibles, etc., with Muslims?

5. To be of real help to the dreamer, what must the Christian friend need to understand most completely when discussing a dream or vision experience?

CHAPTER 7

What the Bible Says About Dreams and Visions

One of these days some simple soul will pick up the Book of God, read it, and believe it. Then the rest of us will be embarrassed. —Leonard Ravenhill

One night during the second year of his reign, Nebuchadnezzar had such disturbing dreams that he couldn't sleep. He called in his magicians, enchanters, sorcerers, and astrologers, and he demanded that they tell him what he had dreamed. As they stood before the king, he said, "I have had a dream that deeply troubles me, and I must know what it means." —Daniel 2:1-3 NLT

Then, after doing all those things, I will pour out My Spirit upon all people. Your sons and daughters will prophesy. Your old men will dream dreams, and your young men will see visions. —Joel 2:28 NLT.

DREAMS AND THE BIBLICAL WORLDVIEW[1]

It is evident to the careful reader that the Bible, in both Old and New Testaments, contains numerous accounts of dreams and visions. In contrast to the Western worldview that has all but reduced the role of dreams and visions to the realm of parapsychology, the men and women of Scripture regarded dreams and visions as a natural, even expected, course of life. Frieda Fordham comments in her book on Jung's psychology that:

...to ancient man the dream was sent by God, and while the Church still allows this possibility (only very cautiously, and reserving to itself the right to adjudicate in the matter), popular opinion to-day has deprecated this kind of psychic activity to such an extent that it is often believed that dreams are merely the result of physical causes, such as sleeping in an uncomfortable position, or eating a heavy meal before going to bed.[2]

And as such, any apparent "message" that a dream or vision might pretend to convey is effectively meaningless. In contrast, the Bible records as reality a world in which dreams and visions operate as one of the legitimate channels of divine, personal revelation. According to Bernard Ramm, in his book dealing with special revelation, dreams and visions can be used as means of divine revelation that are "accommodated to man, his language, his culture and his powers."[3] Ramm continues:

A dream, for example, is one of the cosmic (means) of revelation. Dreams are common experiences of men. But because dreams are common experiences they are drawn into the complex of revelation. The dream bears the structure of laminated wood. On the top side it carries the divine truth; on the bottom side it is a typical human experience. Yet the revelation-bearing dream forms a unity we cannot divide up without destroying its reality. Or to put it another way, by means of the dream special revelation comes within the human orbit in an authentic manner. But it is special revelation coming into the human orbit so that the dream carries this as precious cargo.

Therefore we are not confronted with the dream-in-itself, as if dreams themselves had revelation-bearing powers. Nor are we confronted with revelation-in-itself, as if revelation could reach our consciousness separate from any medium. The dream becomes revelation-bearing when God in His grace so sanctifies it and uses it to this purpose; and the Word of God in special revelation truly comes to us when

God chooses to send it to us by the use of some cosmic conductor.[4]

Thus Ramm concludes that dreams and visions are not only potential conduits of divine communication but in actuality, are often sanctified means of special (and normative) revelation that God uses to warn, direct, or encourage someone. He notes further that:

> Dreams occur in the service of revelation from Genesis to Acts. The "Redeemed" (Joseph and Daniel) and "Unredeemed" (Pharaoh, Nebuchadnezzar) both experience them. In the dream the human mind is the screen upon which the divine revelation is reflected. Because the dream is part of the anthropic and mediated revelation the dreamer dreams within the schemata of his own culture and its symbols. The special revelation does not deliver a man out of his historical and cultural connections. Thus Joseph's dreams are Palestinian, Pharaoh's Egyptian and Daniel's Mesopotamian.[5]

One of the difficulties the Western Christian has in reading the biblical accounts of dreams and visions is the fact that he has been conditioned to relegate dreams and visions solely to the psychological framework of the dream event (the emotional condition of the dreamer together with the prevailing circumstances). However, the Bible offers no such psychological commentary along with its dream and vision accounts. The men and women of the biblical period simply have dreams and visions and respond to them directly, apparently without considering the possibility that these extraordinary incidents could be mere illusion or irrelevant.

Again, Ramm comments that though dreams are natural phenomena, the revelatory experience for which they are sometimes employed, though unusual, is not somehow unnatural or counter to normal psychology. He notes:

> The use of dreams is unusual in that it involves the divine control of the complex structure of the human mind. On the psychological side, the dreamer is passive and thus a very proper recipient of a divinely given revelation. But any study of the dream from a psychological or symbolic

perspective is not germane to special revelation, for in special revelation this rather ordinary experience is caught up into extraordinary service. As with any (means) of special revelation, man enters (it) normally from his side, yet because God enters it from His side, it immediately takes on a supernatural aspect. Because God does enter the dream- (event) from His side, the dream is a dependable (means) in the service of divine revelation and the knowledge of God.[6]

That God can communicate with man through the complex human psycho/physiology without doing violence to his ordinary psycho/physiologic functions is a testimony to the revelatory intent of God. To this Boyce Bennett agrees:

…when the visionary process (i.e., dreams and visions) is seen as something that can be understood within the limits of what God has already created in the human brain and mind, the mystery (i.e., "How can man experience the divine in his dreams/visions?") has certainly not been eliminated. The mystery actually lies in the "equipment" that God has already created to be at His disposal when He wants to reveal Himself.[7]

Bennett further argues that a study of the dream and vision accounts of Scripture that seeks only to define their parapsychological conditions and implications must fall short. For, he notes:

…parapsychology is concerned with whether or not there is an objectively verifiable paranormal occurrence. Since the events described in the Bible are so distant in both time and space, neither scholars nor parapsychologists have access to objective data that would help to decide such a matter. The investigation, consequently, must be a psychological investigation of the account of what may or may not have originally been a paranormal event.[8]

Though Bennett appears to leave room for the conclusion that the biblical dream and vision accounts may not have had their origin in actual events, he is correct in noting that all that is left for the analyst to evaluate are the biblical accounts themselves.

Given that the Bible records numerous dream and vision accounts throughout both Old and New Testaments, one question begs to be answered: Does God still utilize them in communicating with humankind? Is it valid to suggest that despite the fact that the canon of Scripture is closed that God still speaks to individuals through dreams and visions? One of the key texts that relates directly to this issue is Hebrews 1:1-2:

> *God, after He spoke long ago to the fathers in the prophets in many portions and in many ways, in these last days has spoken to us in His Son, whom He appointed Heir of all things, through whom also He made the world.*

Here it is clear that with the advent of Jesus, something new and vastly superior in divine communication has taken place. What remains to be answered however, is, does God's communication in and through Jesus Christ replace and therefore invalidate all other forms of divine communication? Specifically, does God's revelation of Himself in and through Jesus Christ make the phenomena of divine personal revelation via dreams and visions outmoded, and no longer viable?

To answer these questions it must be noted that the text specifically compares the revelation of God in Jesus with the manner of revelation God provided through His prophets in times past. As will be shown in detail in the following section, God communicated extensively with His prophets through dreams and visions. So it could be argued that what God is in fact replacing with the coming of His Son is any dependence upon divine supernatural psychical experience as a means of knowing divine truth. So now that Jesus has come, all that humankind needs of divine knowledge can be perceived directly in and through Christ.

However, the larger context of the Book of Hebrews does not support such a view. Following the remaining introduction in chapter 1, verse 3, the author of Hebrews begins to establish the greatness of Jesus Christ by demonstrating His superiority over other highly regarded religious entities. First, Christ is shown to be superior to angels (see Heb. 1:4).

Next, He is shown to be superior to Moses (see Heb. 3:3-6). Third, He is shown to be superior to the high priest (see Heb. 7:23-27), and so it continues throughout much of the book. Clearly the emphasis is on Christ's superiority, but to say that this superiority also implies that He has displaced that which He has been compared to is, however, not warranted. For if that were the case, Christ would have done away with the ministry of angels, He would have destroyed the role of Moses (and the Law), and He would have eliminated the office and service of the high priest; something He clearly did not do.

Instead, Christ's life was marked by the ministry of angels from before His birth to the resurrection.[9] He stated early on in His earthly ministry that He had not come to destroy the Law but to fulfill it (see Matt. 5:17). And, as the remainder of Hebrews 7 shows, instead of eliminating the role of the high priest, Jesus assumed the role Himself that He might fulfill it perpetually! (See Hebrews 7:24-28.)

Therefore, on the basis of Hebrews 1:1-2 it can be concluded that far from destroying the means of God's previous communication, Jesus, being far superior, fulfills them by providing a firsthand view of the subject matter of which, and on whose behalf, the Old Testament prophets spoke. Dreams and visions therefore retain their role as vehicles of divine personal revelation, but now the object of their revelatory content, Jesus, is clearly seen.

One final issue related to the continuing nature of dreams and visions as means of personal revelation is the relationship of these events and their messages to the statement of revelatory finality in Revelation 22:18-19, which says:

> I testify to everyone who hears the words of the prophecy of this book: if anyone adds to them, God will add to him the plagues which are written in this book; and if anyone takes away from the words of the book of this prophecy, God will take away his part from the tree of life and from the holy city, which are written in this book.

Is divine supernatural revelation received via dreams and visions in conflict with the finality of biblical revelation and the close of the canon? To say yes would of course challenge the evangelical conviction that holds that new, divine revelation is no longer granted by God: a conviction based upon biblical texts (such as Rev. 22), which demonstrate that God is no longer providing new revelation. To say no requires that spiritual messages conveyed by dreams and visions not be considered "new revelation" in the sense that they bring new, previously un-disclosed material about God, humankind, or the spiritual world, but rather that they announce and apply previously revealed and recorded content of biblical truth to the individual.

Therefore, if we are to consider the messages found in dreams and visions as a "word from the Lord" and consistent with the Christian faith, then the content of these apparently divinely originated experiences must be judged by Scripture. In order for the dream or vision experience then to pass the test of trustworthiness, it must be in agreement with the contents of the closed biblical canon[10] in directing the dreamer toward the God of the Bible according to its recorded plan of salvation.

The texts of both the Old and New Testaments contain numerous accounts of both dream and vision events. Interestingly, though the historical time of reference spans several thousand years from Genesis through Revelation, there remains a fairly consistent view of dream and vision phenomena throughout. What is remarkable with regard to our investigation of the role of these types of experiences in Islam is that the biblical dreamers and the Muslim dreamers share a common attitude toward the dream or vision event and its message!

First, dreams and visions are understood as legitimate means by which humankind receives instruction (information, warning, or direction) from God.

Second, the content of these dream and vision experiences, when properly interpreted, is understood to have undisputed relevance (though some dream or vision accounts relate to future events).

Finally, the dream or vision demands some kind of response. In this sense, dreams and visions are not sent by God simply to instruct the dreamer, but to motivate him to do something. A discussion summary of this general and consistent attitude toward dream and vision events follows.

Dreams and Visions in the Old Testament

In the Old Testament, one of the first biblical characters to receive divine input through dreams and visions was Abraham. In Genesis 12:1 Abram is instructed to leave his country, kindred, and his father's house to go to the land that God would show him. Though it is not explicitly described as such, further accounts of divine instruction suggest that this directive was delivered to Abram through an audition (which fits the general category of vision, it being an audible form of personal revelation).

Later, in Genesis 15:1, following Abram's victory over the five Mesopotamian kings, God provided personal encouragement and confirmation of the covenant promises to Abram through a vision (again, this could have been another auditive experience in which God spoke to Abraham apart from any accompanying physical representation). Finally, in Genesis 20, as Abraham and his family travel toward the Promised Land, God utilized dreams to protect Abraham's wife Sarah from the nuptial designs of Abimilech, King of Gerar.

Following relatively brief dream events in Jacob's life (relative to the Jacob-Laban livestock ownership encounter found in Genesis 31:10-13), dreams and visions as a means of divine instruction are highlighted in the life of Abraham's great-grandson, Joseph. Genesis 37 contains the accounts of Joseph's dreams of his superiority over his brothers, which resulted in their resentment and ultimate disposal of him. Genesis 40 records the account of Joseph's gift of dream interpretation on behalf of his fellow prisoners. In Genesis 41 Joseph is called upon to interpret a dream of Pharaoh that resulted in Joseph's release from prison and ultimate rise to a position of authority.

As Israel's history advances, dreams, and visions play a role in governing the nation. While under the rule of the judges (see Judg. 7), Gideon receives courage to lead Israel into battle against the Midianites on the basis of a dream that he overheard being discussed between two of his enemies. In First Kings 3, God comes to Solomon in a dream to inquire what he would request of the Lord to aid him in reigning over Israel. In First Kings 9, God comes to Solomon again by dream to confirm His response to Solomon's request that Israel enjoy the perpetual blessing of God.

However, as far as the Old Testament is concerned, the most prominent use of dream and vision events occurs in the lives of the prophets. Isaiah, Jeremiah, Ezekiel, Daniel, Amos, Obadiah, Nahum, and Habakkuk all include dream or vision accounts in their writings. It was apparently widely understood that prophets regularly received their information and words of warning from dreams and visions. In keeping with the standards of prophetic office, prophets were required to report only those dreams and visions that were from the Lord, and to do so accurately. Jeremiah records God's displeasure with those prophets who disregarded their prophetic responsibility and instead used their position for their own advantage. He notes:

> Then the LORD said to me, "The prophets are prophesying falsehood in My name. I have neither sent them nor commanded them nor spoken to them; they are prophesying to you a false vision, divination, futility and the deception of their own minds" (Jeremiah 14:14; cf. Jeremiah 29:8-9).

In a similar condemnation of false prophesy, Ezekiel records these words of the Lord directed at those prophets who misrepresented Him:

> Thus says the LORD GOD, "Woe to the foolish prophets who are following their own spirit and have seen nothing." … They see falsehood and lying divinations who are saying, "The LORD declares," when the LORD has not sent them; yet they hope for the fulfillment of their word. Did you not see a false vision and speak a lying divination when you said, "The LORD declares," but it is not I who have spoken? Therefore, thus says the LORD GOD, "Because you have spoken falsehood and seen a lie, therefore behold, I am against you," declares the LORD GOD (Ezekiel 13:3,6-8).

In addition to direct judgment leveled against those prophets who misused their prophetic office, God used the withdrawal of dream and vision events as a form of judgment on Israel, resulting in a period in which God did not directly communicate with His people. Micah prophesied of this coming silence as a result of the continuing evil perpetrated by Israel's prophetic community:

Thus says the LORD concerning the prophets who lead My people astray; when they have something to bite with their teeth, They cry, "Peace," But against him who puts nothing in their mouths, they declare holy war. Therefore it will be night for you without vision, and darkness for you without divination. The sun will go down on the prophets, and the day will become dark over them. The seers will be ashamed and the diviners will be embarrassed. Indeed, they will all cover their mouths because there is no answer from God (Micah 3:5-7).

In a similar vein, Amos prophesied saying:

"Behold, days are coming," declares the Lord GOD, "When I will send a famine on the land, not a famine for bread or a thirst for water, but rather for hearing the words of the LORD (Amos 8:11).

Clearly, the Lord held His prophets to a high standard for the proper use of dreams and visions in the exercise of their prophetic office. Deviation from the truth or making use of such experiences to pursue one's own personal agenda was met by divine sanction that could ultimately cost the prophet his life.

Of all the prophets mentioned, the Book of Daniel records the greatest number of dream events. In chapter 2, Daniel is called upon to interpret the dream of Nebuchadnezzar, King of Babylon. As a result, Daniel is promoted to a position of prominence. In chapter 4, Daniel is again summoned to interpret a dream for Nebuchadnezzar. In chapter 5, Daniel is called upon to interpret the handwriting on the wall directed against Nebuchadnezzar's son and newly appointed King Belshazzar. In chapter 7, Daniel himself has a dream in which four kingdoms of the world (one present: Babylon, and three future) are depicted as wild beasts. Interestingly, despite the importance of this dream Daniel tells no one.

Without explanation, the remaining accounts of personal revelation in Daniel are all referenced as visions. In chapter 8, Daniel has a vision that provides additional detail to the kingdoms depicted in his earlier dream. In Daniel 9:1[11] Daniel has another vision, this one describing the seventy weeks of tribulation that is to be experienced by the nation of Israel before ultimate deliverance will come. In chapter 10, Daniel records the content of his final vision, the glory of God.

Two of the minor prophets' writings, which carry their own names Obadiah and Nahum, are the written record of visions they received. Both deal with an explicit description of judgment on Israel's enemies. Obadiah describes God's imminent judgment of Edom. Nahum describes God's judgment of Nineveh.

The prophet Ezekiel was the recipient of a number of visions throughout his life and ministry. As a prophet of Israel during the Babylonian captivity, Ezekiel's message was threefold: to explain the cause for Israel's current exile; to declare God's future judgment of the nations; and, to proclaim God's future restoration of Israel. Ezekiel's visions included a revelation of the glory of God (see Ezek. 8), a depiction of the wickedness of Judah (see Ezek. 11), and the restoration of Israel (see Ezek. 40-48) as depicted in the reestablishment of the Temple and all its accompanying rituals.

In summary, dreams and visions played an important role throughout Israel's Old Testament history. From Abram's initial call through to the prophets serving during Israel's exile, dreams and visions were consistently used by God to give instruction, warning, and to provide information about coming events. The dream and vision accounts in the Old Testament make it plain that the recipient of the God-given dream or vision did not need to have a religious vocation in order to have such an experience (for example, Amos).

In some cases, God even utilized the dream or vision event to communicate with those in opposition to His people (for example, Abimilech and Nebuchadnezzar). In addition, it is interesting to note that on more than one occasion God provided His servants with a vision of His own glory (for example, Isaiah and Ezekiel) to aid them in the execution of His prophetic declaration. Taken all together, it is clear that the Old Testament worldview clearly embraces dreams and visions as legitimate forms of personal revelation. Through these means of revelation, the transcendent God becomes imminent to direct the affairs of humankind, in and through them.

DREAMS AND VISIONS IN THE NEW TESTAMENT

Following the close of the Old Testament, marked by the words of the prophet Malachi, nearly 400 years passed during which God was "silent." This silence, which had been prophesied by both pre-exilic and exilic prophets as a sign of God's judgment on Israel, comes to an abrupt end in the first few paragraphs of the New Testament Gospel accounts. Matthew[12] and Luke[13] both record dream or vision events that accompany the birth of Jesus Christ. Furthermore, at Jesus' baptism, prior to the beginning of His earthly public ministry, Matthew 3:17, Mark 1:11, and Luke 3:22 all record the auditive event[14] in which the Father declares, *"Thou art My beloved Son, in Thee I am well-pleased."*

Following the birth narratives and introduction to Jesus' earthly ministry, dreams and visions do not play a significant role during the life of Christ on earth. In fact, the only reference to dream or vision events that occur sometime after those noted previously, occur near the end of His life and include the Transfiguration (see Matt. 16:28–17:9; Mark 9:1-9) and Jesus' trial before Pilate (see Matt 27:19, Pilate's wife's dream of warning). Apparently, Christ's bodily presence precluded the need for the use of such a vehicle of personal revelation.

However, as the chronology of the New Testament advances, the occurrences of dream and vision events return, and it is in the Book of Acts that the bulk of the remaining dream and vision events mentioned in the New Testament, outside of the Gospels, occur.[15] In addition, Acts provides the only biblical accounts of the occasion of a dream or vision event that contributes to the conversion of an individual. The following dream or vision events are recorded in Acts:

1. Peter's quotation of Joel 2 that restates the prophetic announcement that in the last days God will pour out His Spirit resulting in prophesy, visions, and dreams (see Acts 2:17).

2. Saul's conversion on the road to Damascus (see Acts 9:3-6) and Ananias' accompanying vision directing him to serve as the instrument of God's mercy to Saul (see Acts 9:10-12).

3. Cornelius' angelic vision (see Acts 10:3) and Peter's related vision of clean and unclean food (see Acts 10:10-16).

4. Paul's invitation to come to Macedonia (see Acts 16:9).

5. Paul's encouragement to remain in Corinth and boldly preach the gospel (see Acts 18:9).

The final account of a dream or vision event in the New Testament is recorded in the Revelation of Jesus Christ to the apostle John. In relation to other New Testament dream and vision accounts that deal primarily with the contemporary setting and issues, the visions of the apostle John, which became the Book of Revelation, stands alone. In its often repeated symbolic images and themes of judgment and restoration, the Book of Revelation resembles the apocalyptic imagery detailed by many of the Old Testament prophets.

As in the Old Testament, the New Testament inclusion of dream and visions events confirm the reality and viability of such as an instrument of God to motivate people, both believers and unbelievers, to respond to divine instruction. The premise that God communicates via dreams and visions to motivate people to respond, gives rise to the central question of this book: Does God make use of dreams and visions to motivate people to make the ultimate, spiritual response—repent and believe? An initial response to this question can be found in the Book of Acts, in which is recorded at least two incidents of dream and vision experiences that appear to contribute to the conversion of one or more individuals.

The first and perhaps most important account of a dream or vision event contributing to conversion is found in Acts 9 and involves the conversion of Saul. Luke records the event as follows:

> *Now Saul, still breathing threats and murder against the disciples of the Lord, went to the high priest and asked for letters from him to the synagogues at Damascus, so that if he found any belonging to the Way, both men and women, he might bring them bound to Jerusalem. As he was traveling, it happened that he was approaching Damascus, and suddenly a light from heaven flashed around him; and he fell to the ground*

*and heard a voice saying to him, "Saul, Saul, why are you per-
secuting Me?" And he said, "Who are You, Lord?" And He
said, "I am Jesus whom you are persecuting, but get up and enter the city, and it will be told you what you must do." The men
who traveled with him stood speechless, hearing the voice but
seeing no one. Saul got up from the ground, and though his eyes
were open, he could see nothing; and leading him by the hand,
they brought him into Damascus. And he was there three days
without sight, and neither ate nor drank (Acts 9:1-9).*

Though little detail is given relative to Saul's thought process during
and immediately following this event, especially during his stay in Damascus, in later references to this event Paul indicates that it was clearly the
pivotal moment of his life.

For instance, in Acts 22:1-21 Paul gives a defense of his teaching and
supposed defilement of the Temple (because of his association with Gentiles) before a riotous mob in Jerusalem outside the Temple. In his dis-
course before the crowd in Ephesus, Paul makes much of his encounter
with Christ on the road to Damascus. And he does so because this event
was singularly important in the radical transformation of his life symbol-
ized by the change of his name from Saul to Paul.

Later, in Acts 26:12-21 in his defense before King Agrippa, Paul again
appeals to the Damascus road encounter to demonstrate to the king that
he had not simply rearranged his life on the basis of someone's irrefutable
argument. Rather, Paul argues, the transformation of his life, from that of
a persecutor of Christianity to a promoter of such, was the result of a direct encounter with Jesus Christ Himself. In Galatians 1:11-17, Paul again
makes reference, albeit veiled, to this encounter with Jesus. In this passage,
Paul indicates that it was this Damascus road vision that marked the time
in history that God was pleased to reveal Himself to Paul.

The incident, recorded by Luke in Acts 9, clearly fits the category of a
vision in that it occurred while Paul was awake. From the account, we learn
that Paul was in fact on a mission to persecute the Church by soliciting
authority from the high priest to seize and transport believers he would

discover in Damascus. It is while Paul is in transit to the high priest that Jesus confronts him through a vision. Based upon the categories of dream and vision events described previously in Chapter 6, this experience of Saul's seems to fit the moral warning category. For in this encounter, Jesus confronts Saul by revealing to him what in reality he is accomplishing through his persecution of the Christians—Saul is injuring the very One, Jesus, he is intending to serve.

From his epistles we learn that Paul had an extensive knowledge of the Scriptures, trained as he was as a Pharisee at the feet of Gamaliel (see Acts 22). As a Pharisee, in contrast to the Sadducees,[16] Paul would have been in agreement with the biblical concept of resurrection and angels (see Acts 23:7-8) and would, conceivably, therefore be open to revelatory messages delivered through the modes of dreams and visions (as this was the dominant means by which angels communicated with men and women, see Matt. 1:20-24). In fact, when the encounter with Jesus is complete, Paul never returns to question the validity or reality of what he had just experienced.

Rather, Paul uses every opportunity to identify that it was just such an experience that changed his life. Had there been in Paul a reluctance to accept his encounter with Christ as genuine, it is doubtful that it would have had such a lasting impact upon his life. And finally, the proof of the reality of Paul's experience to those who doubted was provided without apology in the day-to-day living out of Paul's transformed life: *"I was personally unknown to the churches of Judea that are in Christ. They only heard the report: 'The man who formerly persecuted us is now preaching the faith he once tried to destroy'"* (Gal. 1:22-23 NIV).

While Saul remained in Damascus sorting out the events of his encounter with Jesus, another individual, Ananias, had a vision that challenged him to find and introduce Saul (now Paul) to the Church. Acts 9:10-19 describes the recruiting of Ananias as an envoy from God to Saul. In his vision, Ananias is informed that Saul is the Lord's chosen instrument and despite the fact that Saul had come to Damascus to do violence to the Church, Ananias had been chosen to contribute to Saul's reformation and assimilation into the Body of Christ.

Following Ananias' visit, Saul remained with the disciples in Damascus and began to proclaim that Jesus was the Son of God, the very Christ, to the consternation of the Jews (see Acts 9:19b-22). By the time Luke's narrative reaches this point, it is clear that Saul has undergone a conversion, that he had gone from one who was "breathing threats and murder against the disciples of the Lord" (see Acts 9:1) to one who promoted the name and cause of Jesus Christ as the Messiah is telling. What is lacking in the narrative, however, is information that describes exactly how the conversion took place.

In his commentary on the Book of Acts, Hans Conzelmann remarks that, "Paul (Saul) does not learn of the gospel in the vision itself.[17] He is instead directed to the Church, which is the mediator of this teaching."[18] That this may be so is all but confirmed by Paul himself when in his defense before the crowd in Jerusalem (see Acts 22) he says that when he (Ananias, the representative of the Church) came in response to his own vision to visit Saul, Ananias instructed him to, "*Get up and be baptized, and wash away your sins, calling on His* [Jesus] *name*" (Acts 22:16).[19]

Encounters With Christ

What is instructive from the events in Paul's life for the role of dreams and visions in Muslim conversion is the illustration of the tremendous impact that a dream or vision event can have on an individual. At the time of his vision encounter with Christ, Saul was on his way to Damascus to persecute Christians. In fact, Saul was so convinced of his negative view of Christians and Christianity that he believed he was faithfully defending his Jewish faith by persecuting them (see Acts 26:9-11).

Saul's conversion account makes it clear that dreams and visions used of God for the purposes of salvation do not necessarily require prior faith or agreement with God. Before the vision incident, Saul was intent on finding, arresting, and handing over Christians to the Jewish authorities—actions that were clearly motivated by a failure to understand God's Word.

Second, this incident demonstrates that God can penetrate even the hardest heart by motivating him to consider his spiritual need by heightening his perception of ultimate issues and bring him to Himself. Last, Saul's visionary encounter demonstrates that those dream and vision events used of God that call for a response to ultimate spiritual issues are necessarily comprised of directives and symbolic content that are in agreement with the Scriptures and, in particular, with God's plan for salvation by faith in Christ. Thus, Saul did not receive a message asking him to make more sacrificial offerings in the Temple or work harder at keeping the Law, but to look to Christ.

Following Saul's conversion, the next significant vision episode that contributes to the conversion of an individual is found in the account of the parallel visions seen by Cornelius and the apostle Peter in Acts 10:1-22. Luke records the event as follows:

> *Now there was a man at Caesarea named Cornelius, a centurion of what was called the Italian cohort, a devout man and one who feared God with all his household, and gave many alms to the Jewish people and prayed to God continually. About the ninth hour of the day he clearly saw in a vision an angel of God who had just come in and said to him, "Cornelius!" And fixing his gaze on him and being much alarmed, he said, "What is it, Lord?" And he said to him, "Your prayers and alms have ascended as a memorial before God. Now dispatch some men to Joppa and send for a man named Simon, who is also called Peter; he is staying with a tanner named Simon, whose house is by the sea." When the angel who was speaking to him had left, he summoned two of his servants and a devout soldier of those who were his personal attendants, and after he had explained everything to them, he sent them to Joppa.*
>
> *On the next day, as they were on their way and approaching the city, Peter went up on the housetop about the sixth hour to pray. But he became hungry and was desiring to eat; but while they were making preparations, he fell into a trance; and he saw the sky opened up, and an object like a great sheet coming down, lowered by four corners to the ground, and there were in it all kinds of four-footed animals and crawling creatures of the earth and birds of the air.*

A voice came to him, "Get up, Peter, kill and eat!" But Peter said, "By no means, Lord, for I have never eaten anything unholy and unclean." Again a voice came to him a second time, "What God has cleansed, no longer consider unholy." This happened three times, and immediately the object was taken up into the sky. Now while Peter was greatly perplexed in mind as to what the vision which he had seen might be, behold, the men who had been sent by Cornelius, having asked directions for Simon's house, appeared at the gate; and calling out, they were asking whether Simon, who was also called Peter, was staying there.

While Peter was reflecting on the vision, the Spirit said to him, "Behold, three men are looking for you. But get up, go downstairs and accompany them without misgivings, for I have sent them Myself." Peter went down to the men and said, "Behold, I am the one you are looking for; what is the reason for which you have come?" They said, "Cornelius, a centurion, a righteous and God-fearing man well spoken of by the entire nation of the Jews, was divinely directed by a holy angel to send for you to come to his house and hear a message from you."

Luke records in what remains of Acts 10 that Peter made his way to Cornelius, preached the gospel to those who were gathered in Cornelius' home, and observed the conversion and subsequent outpouring of the Holy Spirit upon them.

In this instance, the function of the dream and vision served as much to prepare the messenger (Peter) as it did the ultimate recipient (Cornelius and household) of the gospel message. According to Acts 10, the only information Cornelius received in his vision was a confirmation that God had indeed received his alms and prayers and that he was to send for someone named Simon (Peter). Luke provides the reader with no information relative to the content of Cornelius' prayers.

In light of the ensuing events, it is possible that he had been requesting of the Lord someone who could further explain to him who Christ was. If this is the case, the angel's response to Cornelius in verse 4, "...*your prayers and alms have ascended as a memorial before God...*" may indicate that his request was about to be honored. What is both puzzling and conspicuous by its absence in Cornelius' vision is any reference to the content of the gospel that Cornelius ultimately needed.

In contrast, Peter's vision appeared to strike at the very core of his own Jewish identity. Despite his efforts to maintain his commitment to respect Jewish ritual and its associated "clean" status (so he could enter the Temple), he found himself being instructed to eat things considered unclean and therefore forbidden. To add to his confusion, the provocative scene that included the lowering of the unclean beasts and the directive to him to kill and eat was repeated three times, in spite of his protests. And yet, so compelling was the vision and the story told to him by Cornelius' messengers who had been sent to retrieve him, Peter could do nothing but submit to the unfolding drama (though he did not as yet understand what the vision had to do with the rendezvous with Cornelius).

It is not until Peter and Cornelius recount their stories to each other that the significance of their respective visions becomes clear. For Cornelius, his vision was perhaps in answer to his prayer that God would send someone who could explain to him more fully who the Christ was. For Peter, his vision revealed that God intended to extend grace and mercy to those who were not Jews. As the meaning of the visionary metaphor dawned on him, Peter finally admitted that God was "*not one to show partiality, but in every nation the man who fears Him and does what is right, is welcome to Him*" (Acts 10:34b-35).

What is instructive for the role of dreams and visions in Muslim conversion from this account of Cornelius' conversion is the display of God's sovereign orchestration of details and persuasion of even reluctant participants to accomplish His plan of salvation for given individuals. That such dream and vision experiences are exceptional, even extraordinary in nature, in that they occur irregularly and without inducement or coercion from the subject or outside interested parties and yet somehow bring together spiritual resources (Peter and the gospel message) with prepared recipients (Cornelius and his family) goes without saying. Here Cornelius and Peter have complementary dream and vision experiences which simultaneously prepare each to fulfill their part in the divine drama: Cornelius to respond to the gospel and Peter to carry it to him.

Cornelius' conversion demonstrates that dream and vision events used by God for the purposes of salvation do not necessarily provide the complete gospel message. As a result, this incident highlights the necessity of a "Peter" figure who can adequately explain the gospel to the "Corneliuses." Also, this account shows that the dream and vision events do not, in and of themselves, result in salvation. Rather, dreams and visions used of God for salvation are preparatory and motivational in nature and make it possible for the subject to "hear" the gospel. For many, they serve as the ultimate spiritual catalyst that draws upon previous religious information about God as the raw material for the dream and vision experience. As in the case of Saul and Peter, what is remarkable is that the dream or vision experience is used of God to overcome objections to, prejudices against, and unbelief with regard to the person and work of Jesus Christ.

Explaining the Gospel to Muslims

In light of the above, another question arises concerning the dynamics and difficulties of explaining the gospel to Muslims: "Could not God do similar things in preparing the messengers as well as the audience through dreams and visions? Does it not seem that, if God could turn the heart of Saul, a hardened persecutor of the Christian faith, and Peter, a committed adherent of the Jewish faith, that He could turn the hearts of Muslims who are equally committed to opposing Christianity and keeping their own ritual?"

The last vision account that relates to the issue of conversion is Paul's call to Macedonian. Luke records the event in Acts 16:6-10:

> *And they passed through the Phrygian and Galatian region, having been forbidden by the Holy Spirit to speak the word in Asia; and after they came to Mysia, they were trying to go into Bithynia, and the Spirit of Jesus did not permit them; and passing by Mysia, they came down to Troas.*

A vision appeared to Paul in the night: a man of Macedonia was standing and appealing to him, and saying, "Come over to Macedonia and help us."

When he had seen the vision, immediately we sought to go into Macedonia, concluding that God had called us to preach the gospel to them.

This unanticipated turn of events, commonly referred to as Paul's "Macedonian Call," occurred while Paul was in Troas, on the coast of the Aegean Sea in what is now modern-day Turkey, during what is known as his second missionary journey.

In the remainder of Acts 16 through 18:22, Luke records the results of Paul's response to the Macedonian Call. Included is the conversion of Lydia (see Acts 16:14); the casting out of a spirit of divination from a slave girl, the resultant uproar in the town marketplace, and Paul's imprisonment in Philippi (see Acts 16:16-24); the conversion of the Philippian jailer and his household (see Acts 16:25-34); the tumultuous response to Paul's gospel in Thessalonica (see Acts 17:1-9); the receptivity of the gospel in Berea (see Acts 17:10-15); Paul's sermon on Mars' Hill in Athens (see Acts 17:16-31); Paul's introduction to Aquilla and Priscilla in Corinth (see Acts 18:1-3); Paul's conviction to go to the Gentiles (see Acts 18:4-6); Paul's extended stay with the newly formed Corinthian church (see Acts 18:7-11); Paul's respite before Roman authorities (see Acts 18:12-17); and his return trip to Antioch (see Acts 18:18-22).

From a study of these passages, it is clear that Paul's Macedonian missionary enterprise was highly successful. Everywhere Paul went he found individuals eager to hear the gospel he preached and prepared to respond accordingly. As a result of this trip, churches were planted in Philippi, Thessalonica, Berea, and Corinth. With the exception of Berea, personal letters from Paul to these churches became part of the New Testament canon. And it is to these churches that Paul returns in subsequent missionary journeys for the purpose of providing pastoral teaching and encouragement.

In this instance, the vision event recorded in Acts 16 served as an indirect agent of conversion as it directed the messenger, Paul, to those who were prepared to hear and respond to the gospel message. By itself the vision event was ineffectual relative to conversion; nevertheless, in this instance it became an irrevocable part of the initiation of a gospel witness in Macedonia and the establishment of local churches throughout the region.

With regard to gospel outreach to Muslims, this incident compels us to ask if God may not, in a similar fashion, direct missionaries or local Christians to individuals or groups of Muslims whom He has prepared to hear and respond to the gospel—individuals or groups who otherwise would go unnoticed. It seems the answer, if we take the biblical record as an example, is yes.

The New Testament writers followed their Old Testament counterparts in recording the dream and vision events that marked critical events in the life of Jesus Christ and the Church. From the initial angelic visions experienced by Joseph, Mary, and the shepherds, to the visionary missionary directives experienced by the apostles Peter and Paul, God used dreams and visions as vehicles to communicate with His people. The New Testament worldview clearly embraces dreams and visions as legitimate forms of personal revelation. Through these means of revelation, the transcendent God becomes imminent to direct the affairs of men and women in and through them. As Morton Kelsey comments in his book, *God, Dreams and Revelation:*

> These earliest Christians believed that the meaning and purpose of the outer world originated in this nonphysical, spiritual world and was deeply influenced by it. They believed that God speaks and works through this world, using such nonmaterial media as dreams and trances, visions, and appearances of angels. To them this was one of the regular ways in which God works, one which is complimentary to his action through the material world and through history.[20]

From the dream and vision accounts discussed, a number of observations and conclusions can be drawn relative to the role of dreams and visions in conversion as recorded in the New Testament. First of all, dreams and visions seem to occur as unexpected events. In each of the three cases previously discussed, the dream or vision events came unexpectedly to the subjects. Though they lived in a culture whose worldview granted the occurrence of divine intervention via dreams and visions—confirmed by the lack of recorded skepticism, doubt, or public discredit on the part of the subjects or others who heard their stories—there is no indication in any of the accounts that the subjects were in any sense pursuing such an experience. The dreams and visions came upon them apparently according to the Lord's own choosing, and, seemingly without warning. Further, with the exception of the apostle Paul, the New Testament does not record additional dream or vision events for any of these people. Apparently, dream and vision events are intended to be exceptional events that take place according to God's choosing.

Second, those who experience dreams and visions treat them seriously by responding to them. In each of the accounts, the subjects treated the content of the dream or vision events with utmost seriousness. In the case of Saul, his Damascus road encounter caused him to become a promoter of the very faith he had attempted to extinguish. In the case of Peter, he set aside his Jewish social constraints to be led to the house of a Gentile; into which he entered, preached, and observed conversions and the coming of the Holy Spirit upon them. In the case of Paul's Macedonian Call, the apostle and his companions changed their itinerary to take the gospel into a previously unreached area. Clearly these New Testament subjects of dream and vision events viewed their response to these directives of these rare encounters as compulsory.

Third, dreams and visions, despite whatever means they may employ to communicate with the dreamer, curiously, do not include the gospel message. The dream and vision accounts that resulted in conversion did not include the content of the gospel per se, though neither did they offer any alternative. The strict gospel message was provided by others outside of the dream or vision event. In his Damascus road experience, Saul came face to face with Christ, and yet, gospel content as Paul later defines in First Corinthians 15 was not included. In Cornelius' case, neither Peter's nor Cornelius' own vision provided gospel content. The gospel message was subsequently preached by Peter in Cornelius' house.

And in the case of Paul's Macedonian Call, the content consisted solely of an urgent request to bring the gospel to them. Apparently biblical dream and vision events, instead of serving as communication forums of gospel content, are divinely employed to "condition" or prepare the dreamer to respond to the gospel when provided by others. The biblical dream or vision then validates the gospel message while at the same time raising the dreamer's awareness of his spiritual need and setting aside whatever objections or unbelief he previously carried, so that his conscious need for salvation dominates his rejection of it.

Fourth, understanding the meaning of the dream and vision required help from someone else. In each of the dream and vision accounts, a full understanding of the content and message of the experience required the involvement of others, which was often supernaturally arranged. Thus Saul gets the help of Ananias and Cornelius the help of Peter.

From the observations noted a biblical grid for understanding dreams and visions in the context of conversion include the following:

1. Dream and vision events are the product of the unconscious exercise of physiological faculties that may be used of God to communicate to an individual, even to bring that person to the brink of conversion.

2. Dream and vision events used of God (of the Old and New Testaments) for spiritual ends do not require previous faith in God nor agreement with biblical truth. Such is the case for the dreams and visions experienced by Abimelech (see Gen. 20:1-18), Nebuchadnezzar (see Dan. 2:1-45, 4:4-37), Pilate's wife (see Matt. 27:19), and Saul (see Acts 9:1-19).

3. Dream and vision events used of God for spiritual ends are comprised of directives and symbolic content that are in agreement with the Scriptures.

4. Dream and vision events intended to bring an individual to faith in Christ do not include complete gospel content. Instead, they motivate the dreamer to consider his spiritual need by heightening his perception of ultimate issues—life, death, judgment, etc.—with regard to Christ, the gospel, and biblical information in general. A review of dream and visions accounts suggest that

the greater the previous exposure to Christian religious information, the greater the specificity of the dream or vision event.

5. Dream and vision events intended to bring an individual to faith in Christ are not direct causes of salvation. Therefore, in order for salvation of an individual to result from a dream or vision experience, a third-party messenger "outside" the dream or vision event must provide the gospel content that the dream or vision experience has suggested.

6. Dream and vision events used of God for spiritual purposes are non-ordinary means by which God communicates to an individual. That is, dreams and vision events intended to convey spiritual content occur irregularly and without noticeable pattern. The Bible offers no indication that they may be induced, coerced, or otherwise produced by either the dreamer or an enterprising missionary.

ଶ୧ତ୨ଶ୨ତ

Points to Ponder

1. In general, how does the Bible portray dreams and visions? What purposes do they serve?

2. How did those who experienced dreams and visions in the biblical era respond to them? How do you account for their level of receptivity and responsiveness to their dream or vision experiences?

3. What is the relationship between dream and vision experiences and biblical truth? In other words, how does what the dreamer experiences relate to what the Bible says?

4. For those dream and vision experiences concerned with gospel and salvation issues, why do you think that the experience does not include the explicit message of the gospel?

5. What is the role of the Christian friend in helping the dreamer understand and respond to his or her dream or vision experience?

CHAPTER 8

Mohammad or Jesus? Real-Life Stories

Your vision will become clear only when you look into your heart. Who looks outside, dreams. Who looks inside, awakens.
—Carl Jung

And they sang a new song with these words: "You are worthy to take the scroll and break its seals and open it. For You were slaughtered, and Your blood has ransomed people for God from every tribe and language and people and nation. And You have caused them to become a Kingdom of priests for our God. And they will reign on the earth." —Revelation 5:9-10 NLT

Again, these three stories were told to me personally by Muslims who have come to know Jesus through God's use of dreams and visions.

YOUCEF'S STORY

What is the real path that leads one to God? Is it Mohammad and the Qur'an or Jesus and the Bible? Is it the path of my parents and grandparents and of virtually everyone I know around me, or is it the path of those Christians?

I was haunted by these questions and wanted desperately to find an answer. They echoed in my mind when I was alone, they kept me awake at night when I couldn't sleep. The more I searched, the more the questions pressed upon me.

It all started near the end of my junior year in high school. I was 17 and the normal questions of what I was going to do with my life were becoming more frequent from friends and family. I too wondered about it and though I had some ideas, the uncertainty of my future weighed upon me, especially in light of the political instability that reigned in my country, Algeria.

My family was not very religious, at least not in terms of public expression of their faith, but I was increasingly drawn to spiritual things. One day a friend of mine gave me a copy of the Jesus film in the Kabyle language. At the time, it was the only film that existed in my mother tongue. I was thrilled and wasted no time in finding a way to watch it. I was fascinated by the life and words of Jesus—some of which seemed to be faintly familiar. But I was deeply moved by His death and resurrection. I was really bothered that the One who called Himself the Son of God would die like that—on a cross. Despite the fact that I knew what Islam said about the Christian idea of Jesus dying on the cross—that it was rather someone else, someone like Judas who betrayed him and who therefore deserved to die—I couldn't get the images out of my mind.

Sometime later, I was in a café in town sharing coffee with a friend and somehow our discussion turned to spiritual things. To my surprise, my friend began talking about Jesus and, over the course of our conversation, I expressed a wonder and respect for Jesus that had been growing in me ever since I had seen the film. Our conversation went on for hours, and just before I left, my friend slipped me a small book—the New Testament.

Over the next several months, I devoured the New Testament—reading and re-reading the Gospels in particular, always in search of the answer to the question that had been bothering me for months, "What is the real path to God?" The more I read, the more I was confronted by the uniqueness of the life of Jesus that I had seen in the film, and now read in the pages of the New Testament. When possible, I arranged to meet my friend—the one who had given me the New Testament. And each time we got together, I bombarded him with questions.

This went on for months, and then one night I had a dream. In my dream friends from school and several family members appeared. They were speaking to each other and seemed to be acting out a scene from the life of someone I knew. I couldn't clearly hear what they were saying, and it was as if I was watching them by looking in through a window. But when I awoke, I somehow knew that the dream had come from God, and that God was trying to tell me something. But what was He trying to tell me? Was the answer to my question somewhere in the dream?

One beautiful morning several days later, I was at home, and suddenly I saw a vision. In the vision, friends and family were talking and acting out a scene of someone's life. I could not hear all that they were saying and again it was like in my dream, as if I was watching it all happen by looking in through a window. Again, I knew somehow that the vision was of God and that He was trying to tell me something. But again, the vision did not seem to fully answer the question, "Which path leads to God?"

Not many days later, while reading more of the New Testament, I came across John 14:6. In this passage Jesus is responding to Thomas, one of His disciples, who has just asked Jesus how He and the other disciples can possibly know the way, since they have no idea where Jesus is going. Jesus responds, *"I am the way, and the truth and the life; no one comes to the Father, but through me."* Suddenly the truth of Jesus' words broke through to me. Finally here was the answer to the question that I had been asking for months. The path to God wasn't a religion or a formula but a person! I re-read it just to be sure that I understood it, "I am THE way, and THE truth, and THE life…" Quickly and quietly I called out to God, "If this is true, what should I do?"

In the days and weeks that followed, I began to tell members of my family and certain friends at school that God answered my prayer and that Jesus was THE way, THE truth, and THE life. At first my family members didn't take me too seriously. Some of my friends, however, when they heard what I had been reading in the New Testament, when they heard me tell of my dream and vision experiences, and when they heard my answers to their questions, they began to consider the way of Jesus as well.

Finally, I found an opportunity to meet with my friend from the café. I couldn't wait to tell him all that I had read in the New Testament and seen in the dream and vision. I was convinced that all this had happened because God had sent it all to me to tell me something. I was hoping that my friend would confirm what I had discovered that the answer to my question was not a religion or a formula but a person—Jesus.

I was overjoyed when my friend, using the same verse that I had stumbled upon, explained to me that Jesus was indeed the way, the truth, and the life, that Jesus was the answer to my question, "Which path leads to God?" and that the message from the dream and vision was that God wanted me to turn over my life to Him.

The truth of the Word of God broke through to me from John 14:6. Interestingly, since those days, I have gone on to live out the reality of the scenes from my dream and vision. Furthermore, after deciding to follow Jesus as the way, the truth, and life for me personally, I discovered that an Old Testament hero of the faith had experienced the same dream as mine and that he too had lived out the scene from the vision just as it had come to pass in my own life.

After finishing high school, I went to a university where I studied veterinary medicine at first in Algeria and then in France. After some time in France, I felt the "push" of God to change directions and began theological studies with the objective of becoming a pastor and giving to God what He had asked for in my dream and vision—my life. After my theological studies were finished, I remained in France and have served as a pastor in a local church.

෧෯෨෯෨෯෨

ALI'S STORY

With tears streaming down my face, I called out to God in a choked, raspy voice, "Oh God, I believe you are there. I know You hear me now. I am so confused. I do not know if You are God of the Christians or of the Muslims. Please show me the way before I die. I love You and I ask You from my heart to show me." I slumped back down on the couch in the living room of my apartment and waited.

A year or so earlier, I left my homeland of Palestine. I was tired of the constant harassment and the suicide bombers. Life was miserable, and I was always afraid that I would get caught in one of those accidents that ripped open the bodies of fathers and mothers in the markets, or kids on their way to school. Was that what life was supposed to be about? Why couldn't we both, Jews and Arabs, just live together as brothers? Didn't we share the same father, Abraham? Didn't we both claim to follow a religious path?

I was a Muslim, born to a Muslim family in Bethlehem. When I was of age, I began to say my prayers just like my father, and his father before him, and his father before him. I read the Qur'an. I kept Ramadan. I was a good Muslim. But the conflict I saw around me every day bothered me. Though I loved Islam, certain passages from the Qur'an bothered me. Such as this one from Surah 2:191, "Kill them wherever you find them!" I wondered, *Why does God ask us to kill people?*

Pushed by the restlessness in my soul because of the fighting and killing I saw around me, I immigrated to Belgium in 2004. Once I had settled into my new life, I noticed that things were finally quiet. There were no shootings in Belgium. No air raid sirens. No burned out cars or markets destroyed by a bomb from the day before. And in this place of peace, I began a search for Truth. I began to read the Qur'an like I never had before. I collected other books about the Islamic faith and the life of Mohammad the prophet. I searched on the Internet for well-known and reputable sites that could explain the doctrine of Islam. I watched television programs and listened to the radio. I had a hunger to know the truth like a land parched by drought hungers for rain. And what I found shocked me.

When I studied the life of the prophet Mohammad and read about all the wives he had, and one, Aisha, who was so young, I couldn't believe it. When I learned that paradise was described as a sensual retreat where brown-eyed virgins serve the pleasures of men, I couldn't believe it. And I asked myself, "Why didn't I know this before?"

The more I studied, the more disappointed I became. Slowly I slipped into depression. I was 44 years old, married with young children, and living far from my homeland and my family, and now I was coming to the conclusion that I could no longer agree with or follow the religion of my parents. I suddenly felt all alone, abandoned. Not even my wife and kids could fill the hole that threatened to swallow me.

As I sat on the couch, I felt a breeze. The breeze whooshed over me and then I felt something like a current of electricity that ran from my feet to the top of my head. My eyes closed and I couldn't open them, though I was awake. I continued to hear the wind whooshing over me and the electricity coursing through my body, and then a voice spoke to me. "Imad, I will show you the way. Give Me your hand." As suddenly as the wind and electricity came, they left. I opened my eyes and saw no one. But somehow I knew that God had heard my cries.

The next day, I took my son to buy bread, and I happened to pass by a man that I despised. He was from Iran and from the day that I met him, he talked to me of only one thing—Jesus Christ. I couldn't understand it. He was from Iran. And in my mind, he was therefore a Muslim, like me. Why did he insist on talking to me about Jesus, like the Christians do? Because I couldn't understand what he was doing or why he was doing it, I spoke roughly to him and treated him mean so that he would go away and leave me alone. But today, for some reason, when I saw him I felt differently. Instead of pushing past him, I embraced him and I said I was sorry for how I had treated him. He just laughed and said, "I knew sooner or later you would hear from God."

With the help of my new friend from Iran, I began to study the Bible. My hunger for the Truth had found a new pursuit and I fed it with all that I could get my hands on. I ordered three Bibles from sources I found on the Internet. I borrowed and purchased over 50 books on the Bible and the life of Jesus. I listened to the radio and I watched television programs that explained the Christian faith. It was difficult, because I came face to face with teachings that contradicted what I had been taught as a Muslim. But in every instance, the Man from my dream proved Himself faithful—He did guide me. He brought people into my life to answer my questions. He introduced me to others from a Muslim background who also had discovered the Savior Jesus Christ. He answered my prayers and showed that He was alive and interested in me.

And little by little my life is changing. The sadness that I felt has been replaced with happiness. The fear I had has been replaced with peace—I am no longer afraid to die. The hate that was taking over my heart, Jesus has replaced with love.

Recently, I had another dream of Jesus. In this dream, Jesus showed me three people from my family whom I had not seen in a long time, and He told me that I needed to love them. When I saw who He was referring to, I thought, *Oh, no, not them! These people have treated me badly and I really don't want to even try to contact them.*

But in an effort to try to obey the words of Jesus, I called the first man, Mahomed. When he heard my voice, he didn't immediately recognize me, but when I told him who I was he was surprised. And the first thing he said to me was, "Today, I had a dream of Jesus all dressed in brilliant white and He told me to go further and search. And he told me that He is God." And then he asked me, "Ali, can God talk with me?"

A few weeks later, it was Mahomed who called me; this time to tell me that he had just had another dream. And he told me, "In this dream, I saw Jesus sitting beside another man who I didn't recognize and they were talking, but I couldn't hear what they were saying. But I noticed that Jesus was so beautiful, and He was looking right at me as if He wanted to say something to me. And then I woke up. Ali," he asked, "what does it mean? What does Jesus want to say to me?" I told my friend to keep searching, to read the Bible, to call out to God. I reassured him that Jesus would definitely tell him what He wanted him to know.

❖❦❖❦❖

MEHDI'S STORY

"Mehdi! What are you doing there? Hey, Mehdi, do you hear me?" The voice of my friend woke me from my semi-trance, and I turned to face him. He ran across the road toward me and again asked me, "What are you doing in front of the church? You don't want to go in there do you?"

I smiled and said, "Of course not." And I took off with my friend toward downtown. Though I pretended like it was nothing, I have no idea how long I was there in front of the church staring up at the cross that was attached above the huge front doors. I knew that this church in the center of town had been there for a long time. And I often passed by it on my way into town without really ever noticing it. It was a church and that was it. I never had the least interest in knowing more about it nor going inside. The church was the so-called holy place of the Christians and I was a Muslim, even if I wasn't very practicing. However, over the last while, I had become troubled by the cross.

I come from a Muslim family of four children—three girls and myself, the firstborn son. As far as our family is concerned, we were Muslim by tradition more so than by practice, which means that apart from the month of Ramadan during which we tried to do like everybody else, there wasn't much that we did that displayed our Muslim faith. And in fact, religion of any sort didn't interest me in the least.

While I was in high school, I began to ask myself questions concerning what I was going to do with my life. Among other things, I started to investigate the art world, and I discovered my passion for the cinema. With this awareness, I oriented myself toward the study of cinema with the dream of one day becoming a film producer. This decision, together with my first few cinema courses, reinforced my attitude to ignore religion. For in addition to my lack of interest in the subject, I came to understand that in the world of cinema, religion was not very "chic." With this in mind, I dove into this new world and I was happy.

But my contentment did not last long. With a little bit of distance now from these events, I can now see that my life was rocked as the result of a seemingly chance encounter with a young foreigner who lived not far from me. His name is John and for reasons which I still do not fully understand today, each time our paths crossed in our neighborhood, we would stop and exchange a few words. I don't know why. It was never anything of real importance, but it happened seemingly every time we saw each other.

On one of these occasions, after trading pleasantries, John invited me to his house for a Christmas party. Since I didn't have anything else to do, I accepted. The evening came, and I went to John's party. At the party there were a few people I had seen and knew to some extent from the neighborhood. There were also a few people I had never seen before. We ate, and at one point in the evening someone gave a presentation of what Christmas really was all about. That's all. There was nothing shocking about what happened or what was said, but nothing very interesting either. As I left, my friend John gave me a book that I accepted but never even looked at.

One evening several months later, I was home with nothing to do. As was my habit, I turned on the television and flipped through the channels hoping to find a good film. This time I fell upon a religious program featuring a man named Father Botros. Father Botros is a Coptic Priest from Egypt, and his program consists of reading from the Qur'an and then commenting on what he has read, as well as presenting the gospel of Christ. I really was not attracted at all to religion, much less to some old bearded guy reading from the Qur'an! But what caught my attention in the couple of minutes before I flipped over to something else was his way of dissecting the Quranic text and providing an explanation like I had never heard before in my life. His approach set something off inside of me and for the next couple of months I gave myself to the task of confirming what Father Botros said through the study of the Qur'an and books about it. At the end of a few months I concluded that Islam was not the right path. Interestingly I wasn't really shocked by my conclusion. In fact I was actually relieved. Perhaps now religion would go away and leave me alone! But that wasn't to be the case, as I found out next.

Having heard what Father Botros had to say about the Qur'an I could not help but think about what he also said about the Bible—a book I knew absolutely nothing about. Curious, I got hold of a Bible, and I started to read it. To my great surprise what I read began to work on me. And one thing in particular drew my attention—the cross—the cross of Jesus. All of a sudden I began to see the cross everywhere, in the films I watched, in the books I read, in nature as I moved around from place to place, and yes, above the huge doors of the large church in the center of town. All of this began to trouble me. And I asked myself, "Why? Why the cross? Why am I seeing this image everywhere? Why me? I'm not even interested in religion." Following these troubling moments, I visited the national church. Again, I did so more out of curiosity than out of any real interest on my part. And again, I was not very impressed by what I saw and heard. Without really finding any answers to my questions, I turned my back on it all and returned to my life as a student of cinema.

For a while all was well and I was at peace. But then all of that stuff came rushing back, and I found myself once again troubled about the questions of the cross. This time, however, the line of questioning had changed. Instead of asking "why," I found myself asking, "And what if it's true?" I, the one who had adopted the attitude of an atheist and who had done the research to conclude that Islam—the faith of my family and my country— was not the right path; I, who didn't have the least amount of interest in getting my life mixed up with religion, found myself confronted by a reality that I could no longer ignore.

"And what if it is true? What if the cross and the person of Jesus and His teaching from the Bible are true? What does all that mean for me?" The more I tried to push away these thoughts, the more they came to fill and overwhelm my mind. I became nearly paralyzed. I was no longer able to concentrate on my studies. I couldn't stop thinking about these questions, about what I heard from Father Botros, and what I had read in the Bible. I got so worked up that I began to lose sleep and for several nights in a row, I didn't sleep at all.

My crisis hit its crescendo during summer. It was hot, and my family and I were obliged to sleep outside in the inner courtyard of our house, which allowed at least the idea of a cool breeze to wash over us from time to time as we slept. I was really tired and had already spent two nights unable to sleep. And yet, I found myself again unable to sleep—my thoughts fixed on the question, "And what if it's true?" Finally, I couldn't take it any longer, and I cried out, "God, if You are there, give me a sign. Give me a clear sign that will answer all my questions." I lay on my back and looked up at the sky. It was nighttime. It was hot and clear. There was no wind, not even the smallest breeze. There were no clouds and the stars were shining very brightly.

Suddenly I saw something that startled me. Just after I ended my prayer, I saw the stars begin to move. Some from the left and others from the right moved toward each other until they formed the shape of a cross! There in the night sky right over the courtyard of my house. I couldn't believe it. I thought surely I must be imaging things, or perhaps because I was so tired I was hallucinating. I blinked my eyes, I wiped my face with my hands in an effort to wake myself up and clear my head. But I was really awake. And the stars in the shape of the cross stayed where they were. And finally I understood. This is what God had sent me in answer to my prayer. Here was my sign. And for the first time in three nights, I rolled over and went directly to sleep.

The next morning I went to see my friend John from the neighborhood. I told him all that had happened to me. He didn't seem to be too surprised, but rather happy that I had encountered God. Then he took the time to explain to me what the cross signified for Jesus, for himself, and for me. That's when it all came together. After years of my atheistic attitude, years during which I wanted to live my life for me and stay as far away as possible from the annoyance of religion, I understood that a life without the cross of Jesus is not really a life at all. With the help of my friend John, I asked for the forgiveness of my sins and soon after was baptized. God changed my life and I want to live all the rest of it for Him.

ଡ଼୧ଡ଼୧ଡ଼

Points to Ponder

1. How did God begin working in Youcef's life?

2. What prevailing feeling drove Ali to seek after God?

3. What evidence of a changed life do Youcef and Ali describe after their dream experiences?

4. To what extent do you think that Mehdi's conclusion that Islam was not the right path made him potentially more receptive to the gospel? Which system of beliefs do you think is more opposed to the biblical message, Islam or atheism? Why do you think so?

5. How does the role played by the Christian friends who helped Youcef, Ali, and Mehdi understand their dreams in light of the gospel help you understand how you could play the same role for a Muslim friend or colleague?

CHAPTER 9

What's Next?

God is pursuing with omnipotent passion a worldwide purpose of gathering joyful worshipers for Himself from every tribe and tongue and nation. He has an inexhaustible enthusiasm for the supremacy of His name among the nations. Therefore, let us bring our affections into line with His, and, for the sake of His name, let us renounce the quest for worldly comforts and join His global purpose. —John Piper

This man Daniel…has exceptional ability and is filled with divine knowledge and understanding. He can interpret dreams, explain riddles, and solve difficult problems… —Daniel 5:12 NLT

Dreams. Visions. Islam. Christianity. Divine encounter. Miracles. Psychology. Truth. For the Westerner, an examination of the phenomenon of dreams and visions as presented in this book inevitably involves a confrontation of worldviews. And worldviews, as they provide a framework for understanding and evaluating the events, circumstances, and information of life, necessarily lead to defining that which will be accepted as true for a given culture.

With the advance of history, cultures developed tools that enabled them to refine their assessment of the events, circumstances, and information of life that in turn led to inevitable and unpredictable shifts in worldview and its consequent conclusions concerning truth. This shift in worldview that pushed dreams and visions to the periphery of valid spiritual experience for the church in the West is clearly attested to in its history.

But did the philosophical and theological conclusion that dreams and visions were then considered to be off-limits mean that God could no longer employ them for His ends? History has shown that this has not been the case though the Western church, by adopting an anti-dream attitude, effectively shut itself off from the benefits. By preferring to vest all spiritual authority in the church, the church set itself up as the gatekeeper of legitimate spiritual encounter. It became almost as if God could not speak unless He did so through a recognized representative of the church.

Perhaps, had the church only to contend with itself, this restricted platform of divine communication might have been sufficient. With only church people to care for God could have perhaps made effective use of a church-spokesperson-only model to get His message across; assuming of course that everyone in the church was also inclined to listen. But the world in which we live is not comprised of only church people. Most of the world is outside of the church and, in many instances, opposed to the church and its message. Which brings us to perhaps the critical issue of biblical history—how will God communicate with those who stand in opposition to Him? What means will He employ to make clear His divine will?

Though some, like the people of Israel, enjoyed access to Scripture, divine promises, anointed prophets, and miracles that confirmed the divine message, others did not. If God were locked into a church-spokesperson-only model, many who have lived beyond the reach of the church would find themselves also beyond the reach of God's message as well. Is this the case? The Bible says otherwise.

+ *The heavens proclaim the glory of God. The skies display His craftsmanship. Day after day they continue to speak; night after night they make Him known. They speak without a sound or word; their voice is never heard. Yet their message has gone throughout the earth, and their words to all the world…* (Ps. 19:1-4 NLT). God speaks through His creation.

+ *Indeed, the Sovereign LORD never does anything until He reveals His plans to His servants the prophets* (Amos 3:7 NLT). God speaks through His messengers the prophets.

+ *Long ago God spoke many times and in many ways to our ancestors through the prophets. And now in these final days, He has spoken to us through His Son…* (Heb. 1:1-2 NLT). God speaks through His Son, Jesus.

+ *Then, after doing all those things, I will pour out My Spirit upon all people. Your sons and daughters will prophesy. Your old men will dream dreams, and your young men will see visions* (Joel 2:28 NLT). God speaks through supernatural means, including dreams and visions.

Clearly God has not limited Himself to a church-spokesperson-model for making His will known to humankind. As He speaks through the multiplied grace-enabled channels of divine communication, the Church, the Body of Christ, grows and prospers and those outside the Church experience reconciliation as each person welcomes and appropriates the divine message for him or herself.

And this is key for peoples and nations opposed to the God of the Bible such as those under the mantel of Islam for whom access to the biblical message is limited. *"How shall they call upon Him in whom they have not believed? And how shall they believe in Him in whom they have not heard? And how shall they hear without a preacher?"*[1] Such are the questions posed by the apostle Paul in defense of his passion to carry the gospel to the Gentiles—those on the outside with regard to the blessings of God. The answer, of course, to Paul's rhetorical queries: "They can't!" They can't call upon Him in whom they have not believed. They can't believe in Him whom they have not heard. And they can't hear without a preacher! Remarkably for many who find themselves outside the reach of the Church, God Himself is standing in as Preacher, making use of dreams and visions to call people to Himself. Such is the case for many Muslims.

Is the Western Church Ready?

But this brings us to another issue for the West in general and the church in the West in particular: "Is the West ready and able to allow again for the possibility of divine revelation via dreams and visions?" Is the church ready and able to admit that God is at work among Muslims bringing them to Himself through supernatural means? Is the church in the West ready to serve in the role of Christian friend to accompany a Muslim dreamer to understand gospel truth? Finally, is the church in the West ready and able to embrace those who respond to dreams and visions and incorporate them into the life and fellowship of the church? Or will the current anxiety toward Islam prevail and push the church back to medieval attitudes of "us against them"?

If the West has learned anything from the last 1,400 years of history (and that of course remains to be seen), it is that Islam is a neighbor not likely to move away, at least not anytime soon. Efforts on the part of the West—whether governments or the church—to reform, assimilate, or simply annihilate Muslim populations have virtually all met with some level of frustration if not failure, whether one considers the work of men like Peter the Venerable or Ramon Lull on the one hand, or the Medieval Crusaders and the Coalition forces of the first decade of the 21st century on the other.

Despite the conflict, both from within and without, the humiliation of colonizing regimes, and the struggle to modernize without succumbing to modernism, Islam has succeeded in proving itself to be a formidable opponent by establishing itself as a global force once again. And herein lies the irony, that whereas Islam seems to draw its strength from the union of its political and religious agendas and identities, the church in its attempts to do the same succeeds only in revealing its weaknesses. Faced with the rising tide of Islam, what's the church to do?

Though viewed by some during the middle ages as a Christian heresy, few in the church today would associate Islam with anything Christian, despite the commonalities between the two faiths. Islam, for its part, would also distance itself from any admission that it shares anything but prophetic ancestry and religiously outward forms with the people of the Book.[2] It is just this complex web of similarities and differences that the two faiths share that makes Islam so difficult to penetrate with the Christian message.

Both Islam and Christianity hold to a monotheistic expression of God. Both respect and consider divine some of the same Scriptures; though Muslims would add the Qur'an to the list of sacred writings that includes the Torah, the Psalms, and the Gospels that Christians accept. Both understand that God intentionally communicated with humankind, making use of prophets and angels to do so. Both await the return of Jesus, a final day of reckoning and an eternity in paradise for the faithful. With all this and more in common between Christianity and Islam, why then the conflict? On what grounds do either one of these two monotheistic expressions of faith assert its exclusiveness and to what can the suspicion that each has for the other be attributed?

Historically, the church's efforts to encounter and engage Islam varied from dialogue and exchange at an intellectual and spiritual level to armed conflict. Frankly, it seems difficult to understand how the message of Jesus—that He came to love and die to reconcile man to God (and man to man)—could take the form of military conquest. It could be argued, however, that perhaps some of this activity reflected the attitude of the age. The message of Pope Urban II that launched the Crusades ignited a powder keg of spiritual frenzy that took shape in the forming of an army that had as its goal to liberate formerly Christian lands—and in particular, Jerusalem. But his promises of glory to the victorious and forgiveness of sins for those who took part in the cause were not disconnected from prevailing streams of Christian thinking. Pope Urban II simply combined the old idea of pilgrimage to the Holy Land with the more recent idea of holy war against the infidel. The crusader was at once pilgrim and soldier, bound by a solemn vow, attested to by the wearing of a cross sewn to one's clothes, to visit the Holy Sepulcher in the ranks of an organized, armed expedition.[3] But where did this idea of militancy in the name of God come from? What happened to the message of peace and love that Jesus brought?

According to Jacques Ellul, prominent French philosopher and theologian, the influence of Arab thinking on the West was great throughout the 11th and 12th centuries, and not just in matters of philosophy and science. Ellul explains, "It seems that Muslim intellectuals and theologians were much stronger than their Christian counterparts. It seems that Islam had an influence (on Christianity), but not Christianity (on Islam)."[4] How was this influence evidenced? Again, Ellul:

In Islam there was an indissoluble correlation between religious law and political power.... Every political head in Islam is also the ruler of believers. There is no separation of church and political powers. The political head is the religious head. He is the representative of Allah. His political and military acts, etc., are inspired. Now this is all familiar in Europe. The king or emperor does not merely claim to be the secular arm of the church but the one who has spiritual power. He wants to be recognized that he personally is chosen by God, elected by the Almighty. He needs a prophetic word and the power to work miracles. His word and person have to be sacred[5]...In tandem with this great importance of the political power there is, of course, the importance and glorification of war as a means of spreading the faith. Such a war is a duty for all Muslims. Islam has to become universal. The true faith, not the power, has to be taken to every people by every means, including by military force. This makes the political power important, for it is warlike by nature. The two things are closely related. The political head wages war on behalf of the faith. He is thus the religious head, and as the sole representative of God he must fight to extend Islam[6] ...(Remember that) for three centuries (following the death of Christ) Christianity spread by preaching, kindness, example, morality, and encouragement of the poor. When the empire became Christian (under Constantine), war was hardly tolerated by the Christians. Even when waged by a Christian emperor it was a dubious business and was assessed unfavorably. It was often condemned. Christians were accused of undermining the political force and military might of the empire within. In practice Christians would remain critical of war until the flamboyant image of the holy war came onto the scene. In other words, no matter what atrocities have been committed in wars by so-called Christian nations, war has always been an essential contradiction to the gospel. Christians have always been more or less aware of this. They have judged war and questioned it.[7]

…Christians did not invent the holy war or the slave trade. Their fault was to imitate Islam. Sometimes it was imitation by following the example of Islam. Sometimes it was inverse imitation by doing the same thing in order to combat Islam, as in the Crusades. Either way, the tragedy was that the church completely forgot the truth of the gospel. It turned Christian ethics upside down in favor of what seemed to be very obviously a much more effective mode of action, for in the twelfth century and later the Muslim world offered a dazzling example of civilization. The church forgot the authenticity of the revelation in Christ in order to launch out in pursuit of the same mirage.[8]

In other words, one of the influences of Islam on Christianity was the adoption of the thought that religious truth should be defended and extended by the sword. In the end, the Christian faith gave in to the influence of Islam and adopted its methods, marrying political force with evangelistic zeal. The results, history tells us, for both ends were disastrous. If only the church had listened to men like Peter the Venerable, Saint Francis of Assisi, and Ramon Lull.

Increased Responsiveness

Despite the conflict that marred the first few centuries of Christian-Muslim relations, the last 50 to 100 years have seen a significant increase in the responsiveness of Muslims to the gospel. Humanly speaking, to what can this shift in responsiveness be attributed? Several things are evident. First, Islam is getting more attention. The 20th and early 21st centuries were the stage for numerous political and religious events that pushed Islam and Islamic nations and causes into the public forum. To cite just a few: the fall of the Ottoman Empire following Word War I (1918) and the subsequent partitioning of a significant portion of the Middle East by British and French authorities; the establishment of the state of Israel (1948) and the resultant problem of determining a homeland for the Palestinians; the

Arab Oil Embargoes (1967 and 1973-74); the deposition of the Shah of Iran (1979) and the ensuing Iranian Revolution; Iraqi Invasion of Kuwait and the 1st Gulf War (1991); the destruction of the World Trade Center (9/11/2001) and subsequent Invasion of Iraq (2003); and the Invasion of Afghanistan (2001). These and other related incidents focused political and media attention on Islam, putting it on the front pages of newspapers and in top stories of nightly newscasts worldwide. Though non-Muslims had difficulty understanding Islam and the intent and response of Muslims, it was becoming clear that they could no longer be ignored.

The second reason for this change is the response of the church. Despite the largely negative reaction from the West that these incidents provoked, the news also got the attention of the church, which began to rethink its relationship to its Muslim neighbors. As a result, more materials that tell the story of Christianity or recount the conversion of a Muslim to Christianity were developed and made available in more languages. Of particular interest is Campus Crusade for Christ's "Jesus Film," which is a faithful retelling of the life of Jesus as recorded in the Gospel of Luke. Since 1979, the film has been translated into more than 1,000 languages, including Arabic, and has been seen by several billion people, according to the Jesus Film Project Website. Another popular resource is the "More than Dreams" DVD and the Website www.morethandreams.org, which includes reenactments of personal testimonies of five individuals representing Iran, Egypt, Turkey, Indonesia, and Nigeria, each of whom turned from Islam to Christianity as a result of a dream or a vision.

In addition to print and multimedia, the rise of the Internet has spawned hundreds, if not thousands, of Websites and blogs that include or are dedicated to presenting the message of Christianity to Muslims; many of these created and animated by Muslim-converts who are able to use this medium to tell their story and guard their identity. Of significance in this vein is the Website http://www.fatherzakaria.net and the televised program of Father Zakarias Botros, a Coptic Priest considered by al-Qaeda to be "one of the most wanted infidels in the world" and considered by Arabic magazines to be Islam's public enemy #1.[9] In his weekly, 90-minute program that is rebroadcast up to four times a week in the Middle East, Father Botros uses the Qur'an to explain to Muslims the errors, fallacies, and shortcomings of

Islam and, in contrast, explain the message of the gospel and saving faith in Jesus Christ.

Third, the interest in Islam that has come from political and media attention has spawned an interest in mission activity among Muslims. Though exact numbers are hard to come by, reports from mission agencies and Bible colleges and seminaries, which have been the typical training ground for missionaries, indicate that the numbers of those preparing for intentional mission work among Muslims is on the rise. Rick Love, in his article that appeared in the *International Journal of Frontier Missions* in 2000, says, "More missionaries than ever before in history are intentionally seeking to evangelize Muslims. More workers means more sowing, more sowing means more reaping. This unchanging, axiomatic principle describes why we may be on the harbinger of harvest among Muslims."[10]

One can only imagine what the events of the past ten years have done to the interest and responsiveness of Christians to the call to reach Muslims at home and abroad. Furthermore, one additional footnote to this description of the swelling of missionary ranks targeting Muslims, is that for the first time churches from South America and Asia—in particular Brazil and South Korea—are preparing and sending their own missionaries, many to Muslims.

Fourth, as more Muslims respond to the Christian message and mature in their faith, more of these men and women are themselves interested and equipped to take the message of the gospel to their own people. In addition to written testimonies that have been available for decades, late-20th century technologies have opened the doors to Internet and film resources enabling Muslim converts to reach many while guarding their personal identities. Further, the natural progression of mission work necessarily includes the training and equipping of the national believer so that eventually the missionary worker can move on to a new location, leaving the established, mature believers able to effectively care for themselves spiritually and reach others of their own people. Examples of this from around the Muslim world are beginning to be made known.

One of the most significant evidences of this progress comes from the Kabyle region of Algeria. Torn by civil war throughout much of the 1990s, Algeria struggled politically and socially on many fronts. One crisis that occupied the minds of Algerians throughout this period was the conflict between the Kabyle Berbers and the Arabs. For reasons that date back to the invasion of Algeria by Arab Muslims in the 8th century, Arab and Kabyle peoples of Algeria have always maintained a certain distance from each other, due in part to their distinct cultures, language, and religious heritage. Though in the minority with regard to the larger population of Arabs in the country, the Kabyles have always fought to retain their cultural uniqueness, particularly when the Arab-controlled government sought to suppress the use of the Kabyle language and the public expression of Kabyle identity.

When mission activity into Algeria in the 1990s introduced the Jesus film, it came at a time when no other films in the Kabyle language existed. Thrilled to have a film in their own language, Kabyle people flocked to get their hands on a copy of the videocassette. As the Arab-crisis intensified, many Kabyle people became disillusioned with Islam, in whose name much of the conflict was being carried out, some of which particularly targeted Kabyles. This disillusionment with Islam, coupled with the message of Jesus in their own language, led many Kabyles to turn to Christianity. Since the end of the conflict in Algeria, stories of Kabyle conversions and the start-up of churches in the Kabyle region of Algeria have become the focus of numerous articles and commentaries.

One of the most prominent examples of what happened can be summed up by the fact that the largest church in Algeria (weekly attendance in the hundreds) is located in the capital of the Kabyle region in the city of Tizi-ouzou.[11] In addition to the size of the congregation, which makes this church nothing short of exceptional, is the commitment the national leadership has to train, equip, and send out its members to reach their fellow compatriots.

Despite the good news of conversion and church growth in places like Algeria, anxiety and uncertainty dominates Western thinking regarding Islam. In December 2009, the Swiss voted in a referendum to ban the construction of minarets (a tower on a mosque from which the people are summoned to prayer). What motivated this response from the Swiss public that had enjoyed relative peace with its Muslim citizens, at least as compared to some of Switzerland's European neighbors such as France and Germany? One Swiss political commentator put it this way, "Many Swiss are worried about the rise of political Islam and religious rules in Europe that are threatening hard-won rights such as equal rights for women and men, the secular rule of law above religion or the right of each individual to decide for him—or herself. A majority of Swiss voters obviously feels that there are problems with Muslim integration into civil society at the moment. This vague sentiment (has been) fueled by a number of incidents over the last years."[12]

A more dramatic expression of the feelings of some in Europe come from Holland and one of its politicians, Geert Wilders. In 2008, Wilders produced a short film entitled, "Fitna" (Arabic for "disagreement and division among people" or a "test of faith in times of trial"). The film makes use of verses from the Qur'an together with media clips and newspaper cuttings showing or describing acts of violence and hatred by Muslims. Wilders' intent is to demonstrate that the Qur'an motivates its followers to hate all who violate its teachings and that it encourages things like terrorism, anti-Semitism, and violence against women and homosexuals.[13] For his part, Wilders endorses the outlawing of the Qur'an in Holland, a halt to all immigration from Muslim countries (into Holland), the paying of Muslims to leave the country, and the deportation of Muslim "criminals" back to their countries of origin. Furthermore, he has gone on record saying, "I have nothing against Muslims. (It's just that) I have a problem with Islamic tradition, culture, (and) ideology."[14]

RETREAT OR REACH OUT?

Against this political and social backdrop, the questions remain: How will the church respond? Will it join with political agents, compromising or reinterpreting its theology in order to justify some sort of "holy war," in line with the Crusaders? Hopefully the disastrous results of having chosen such a path in the past will make this option untenable. Will the Church retreat from an encounter with Islam and seek to forge some sort of ecumenical truce based upon common ground? Such an option seems magnanimous and in line with Jesus' call to peace and harmony, but it fails to value the biblical uniqueness of the very things that separate Christianity from Islam. A move in this direction in the name of pluralism will only dilute and render powerless the very message of the Gospel. Or will the Church return to its roots, and take up the message of Jesus—the message of God's love that resulted in the supreme sacrifice for the forgiveness of sins that is available to all people? Such a path, it seems to me, is the only one that the church can, in good conscience, embrace. And yet, to do so, will require several significant adjustments to the way of "doing church" that has become so common in the West.

First, a biblical approach to an encounter with Islam will require a serious commitment to the method and message of Jesus that includes serving without respect for reciprocation and preaching the gospel of salvation for the forgiveness of sins through faith in Christ alone. Jesus Himself said that He had come "not to be served but to serve others and to give His life as a ransom for many" (Mark 10:45). What will this look like for the church? First, the church will need to adopt an attitude of service and set aside resources so that it can offer real assistance to Muslim individuals, families, and even countries. Second, the church will have to intentionally invest those resources in the lives of those in need.

One opportunity that may be staring the church in the face now is the Maldive islands. The Maldives is a country that has been under Islamic influence since the 12th century.[15] Efforts to engage the population with the message of Christianity has been difficult as there is no national church and missionary visas are not regularly issued. The Maldives are currently under threat from rising ocean levels. Some scientists predict that if things continue as they have been, the islands may become completely uninhabitable by 2100.[16] Questions: What would happen to the testimony of the church in the eyes of the Moldavian population and government if somehow it were able to mobilize resources and offer assistance to relocate and relieve the loss that may be suffered by many Moldavians? Is the church ready to serve?

As to the message of Jesus, in the message that the angels announced to the shepherds, the essential elements of the gospel are revealed. Luke records the scene:

> *That night there were shepherds staying in the fields nearby, guarding their flocks of sheep. Suddenly, an angel of the Lord appeared among them, and the radiance of the Lord's glory surrounded them. They were terrified, but the angel reassured them. "Don't be afraid!" he said. "I bring you good news that*

will bring great joy to all people. The Savior—yes, the Messiah, the Lord—has been born today in Bethlehem, the city of David!" (Luke 2:8-11 NLT)

The Good News, or gospel, announced by the angels had two components. The first is that a Savior is born—but not just any Savior, the Messiah, the One foretold by the prophets, the One who would save His people from their sins—*that* Savior, was born. The second is that this Good News is for all people. Despite the thinking of some that the gospel was to be restricted to a certain race or class of men and women, the angels' announcement only confirmed what the Bible had been saying all along, God's intent is to bless everyone. This is what Jesus refers to when He sends out His disciples following His resurrection.

In Acts 1, Jesus tells His disciples that they "will be My witnesses, telling people about Me everywhere—in Jerusalem, throughout Judea, in Samaria, and to the ends of the earth." Why? So that people everywhere could benefit from the Good News. This is the same theme that is picked up later by the apostle Paul in his letters to the Romans when he says, *"For I tell you that Christ has become a servant of the Jews on behalf of God's truth, to confirm the promises made to the patriarchs so that the Gentiles may glorify God for His mercy, as it is written: 'Therefore I will praise you among the Gentiles; I will sing hymns to your name.' Again, it says, 'Rejoice, O Gentiles, with His people.' And again, 'Praise the Lord, all you Gentiles, and sing praises to Him, all you peoples.' And again, Isaiah says, 'The Root of Jesse will spring up, One who will arise to rule over the nations; the Gentiles will hope in Him'"* (Rom. 15:7-12 NIV). This message of salvation through faith in Christ alone must become the clear clarion call of the church.

Second, such a biblical encounter will require a willingness to accept suffering as a normal part of the cost—not only for the new believer, but also for the messenger. The church in the West—especially the church in the United States—has spent much of the last century in a historic and geographic bubble that has spared it the pain of persecution. This grace, which has allowed the church to prosper, has also contributed to a shriveling of its theology of suffering. In a penetrating look at the prevailing attitude in the West, John Piper offers this assessment:

There is a mind-set in the prosperous West that we deserve pain-free, trouble-free existence. When life deals us the opposite, we have a right not only to blame somebody or some system and to feel sorry for ourselves, but also to devote most of our time to coping, so that we have no time or energy left for serving others. This mind-set gives a trajectory to life that is almost universal—namely, away from stress and toward comfort and safety and relief. Then within that very natural trajectory some people begin to think of ministry and find ways of serving God inside the boundaries set by the aims of self-protection. Then churches grow up in this mind-set, and it never occurs to anyone in such a community of believers that choosing discomfort, stress, and danger might be the right thing—even the normal, biblical thing – to do.[17]

To the extent that what Piper says is reflected in our personal and church outlook toward pain and suffering, is the extent to which we have overlooked or ignored clear biblical teaching on the subject.

A few examples suffice to make the point:

In fact, everyone who wants to live a godly life in Christ Jesus will be persecuted (2 Timothy 3:12 NIV).

Dear friends, don't be surprised at the fiery trials you are going through, as if something strange were happening to you. Instead, be very glad—for these trials make you partners with Christ in His suffering, so that you will have the wonderful joy of seeing His glory when it is revealed to all the world (1 Peter 4:12-13 NLT).

I have told you all this so that you may have peace in Me. Here on earth you will have many trials and sorrows. But take heart, because I have overcome the world (John 16:33 NLT).

It is time for the church to embrace the fact that "frustration is normal, disappointment is normal, sickness is normal. Conflict, persecution, danger, stress—they are all normal."[18] These things are normal because we live in a fallen world that is waiting for its redemption[19] and they are normal because the Good News is opposed wherever it goes.[20]

But we do not embrace suffering because it is somehow in and of itself redemptive or meritorious or glorious, as is the case in some Eastern thought. Rather, we embrace suffering and pain and hardship because of two objectives: first, suffering and pain and hardship, when endured with patience and for the right reasons, produce godly character in us, things like patience, hope, and endurance;[21] and second, it is only through suffering and pain and hardship that the Good News can be delivered to those living in contexts highly opposed to it. Jesus Himself attests to this near the end of His earthly ministry when He says to His disciples, *"If you belonged to the world, it would love you as its own. As it is, you do not belong to the world, but I have chosen you out of the world. That is why the world hates you. Remember the words I spoke to you: 'No servant is greater than his master.' If they persecuted Me, they will persecute you also. If they obeyed My teaching, they will obey yours also. They will treat you this way because of My name, for they do not know the One who sent Me* (John 15:19-21 NIV).

And third, such a biblical engagement will require an adjustment in the worldview of the Church to make room for divine intervention in the form of dreams and visions. God is at work calling people to Himself from every tribe and tongue and nation so that the vision of the apostle John in his Revelation can be fulfilled. According to the testimonies of men and women from all over the Muslim world, much of what God is doing in the lives of Muslims is sparked by dream and vision encounters.

The church in the West is still struggling to throw off the shroud that Thomas Aquinas pulled over her that has ever since hindered her from seeing and experiencing the fullness of divine, supernatural encounters. For if, as Aquinas posited, all that can be known can only be known through reason and the five senses, then we are indeed cut off from any hope of knowledge and experience of the divine. But if, as the Bible explains and demonstrates, God is actively reaching down into the human realm marked out by time and space, then we can see and experience God in ways which, because they originate in the divine, can go beyond our human understanding.

The writer of Hebrews began his epistle with the briefest of summaries of the history of God's purposeful communication: *"Long ago God spoke many times and in many ways to our ancestors through the prophets"* (Heb. 1:1 NLT). He then continues to explain that with the coming of Jesus, God's communication took an important step forward. No longer would the news or warning come through a prophet, now it would come through Jesus Himself. The King has sent His only Son.

The phenomenon of dreams and visions that leads Muslims to faith in Christ is remarkable, remarkable in their effect as in the lives represented by the stories retold here. Even more so when we consider that each dream or vision that serves this purpose is an event in which the God of Heaven finds a way to enter the conscious or subconscious realm of men and women to deliver them a personal invitation to follow Him. That He is doing this is undeniable. That we can play a part is unbelievable.

〜〜〜〜〜

Points to Ponder

1. How does a church-spokesperson-only model limit God's ability to communicate with people in the church? With people outside the realm of the church?

2. How would you describe your feelings toward Islam? Those of your church? What people, events, and circumstances have contributed to these feelings?

3. To what extent is the "us against them" attitude of the Middle Ages still affecting Western attitudes toward Islam (and Islamic attitudes toward the West)?

4. What are some reasons that Muslims are more responsive than ever before to the gospel?

5. What can you do to cultivate a positive attitude toward Muslims? What can your church do?

Endnotes

CHAPTER 1

1. The writer of this experience is a personal friend who graciously allowed me to use his story. See also Hassanain Hirji-Walji, *Bittersweet Freedom* (Bind-a-Book Publishers, 1993, available from Building Bridges, Inc., Monticello, MN), 102-104.

2. "Migrations of Asians from the West Coast of India to East Africa and their financial role in East African commerce have been central to Uganda's economic, political, and cultural history. Asians have been in Uganda in significant numbers since the late-1800s, though the Indian Ocean trade winds had been bringing Asians to Africa for centuries before. In the late 19th century the British recruited Asians to work on the colonial railroad in East Africa and by 1901, when the railroad was completed, nearly 7,000 Asians lived in what is now Uganda. Despite the horrific conditions in which the Asian workers lived, many remained in East Africa when the work was finished. Most of the remaining Asian's were involved in cultivation of cotton and coffee. In spite of their small numbers (in comparison to black Ugandans), Asians soon came to dominate the cotton ginning businesses around the country." B. Adams and M. Bristow, "The Politico-economic position of Ugandan Asians in the colonial and independence eras," *Journal of Asian and African Studies 13*, (1978), 151-166. As cited by Hemant Shah in "Portable Culture" and *Diasporic Identities: Globalization, Mass Media, and the Asian Community in Uganda*, University of Wisconsin, (2006), 7.

3. *Bittersweet Freedom*, 56.

4. Ibid.

5. *The Four Spiritual Laws* is an evangelistic Christian tract created in 1952 by Bill Bright, founder of Campus Crusade for Christ. Bright wrote the booklet as a means to clearly explain the essentials of the Christian faith concerning salvation. The booklet states that just as there are physical laws that govern the universe, so there are spiritual laws that govern our relationship with God. These laws are:

   God loves you and offers a wonderful plan for your life (John 3:16, John 10:10).

   Man is sinful and separated from God. Therefore, he cannot know and experience God's love and plan for his life (Romans 3:23; 6:23).

   Jesus Christ is God's only provision for man's sin. Through Him you can know and experience God's love and plan for your life (Romans 5:8, 1 Corinthians 15:3-6, John 14:6).

   We must individually receive Jesus Christ as Savior and Lord; then we can know and experience God's love and plan for our lives (John 1:12, Ephesians 2:8-9, John 3:1-8, Revelation 3:20).

   "Since its conception in 1952, nearly 2.5 billion 4 Spiritual Laws tracts have been printed." http://campuscrusadeforchrist.com/about-us/history; accessed September 11, 2010.

CHAPTER 2

1. John L. Esposito, *Islam: The Straight Path* (Oxford: Oxford University Press, 1988), 15.

2. Caesar Farah, PhD, *Islam: Beliefs and Observances*, 4th edition, (Hauppaugue, NY: Barron's Publishing, 1987), 28. According to Farah, "The tribes of Arabia selected for their deities those which best reflected their distinguishing characteristics and aspirations…there were hundreds of such deities in pagan Arabia; the Ka'bah (in Mecca) alone at one time housed three hundred and sixty-seven of them."

3. In A.D. 732, Charles Martel led the Frankish army in victory over the invading Islamic forces lead by Emir Abdul Rahman Al Ghafiqi who commanding approximately 80,000 men. Charles' victory at the Battle of Tours saved Western Europe from the Muslim invasions and was a turning point in European history; http://militaryhistory.about.com/od/army/p/martel.htm; accessed June 1, 2010.

4. Adapted from *A Muslim and Christian in Dialogue* by Badru D. Kateregga and David W. Shenk (Scottsdale, PA: Herald Press, 1997).

5. Adapted from *Islam, the Straight Path* by John L. Esposito.

6. Among the reforms instituted by Ataturk, the following are considered to be those that have defined Turkey ever since:

   1922 – Abolished the Caliphate

   1923 – Established the Republic of Turkey with Ankara as the capitol city

   1924 – Closed religious schools, abolished Shari'at law, adopted constitution

   1925 – Replaced Islamic calendar with Gregorian (Western) one

   1926 – Ended Islamic polygamy and adopted civil marriage

   1928 – Adopted Turkish alphabet (effectively cutting ties to Arabic language and culture)

   1934 – Women given the right to vote; http://www.allabout-turkey.com/reform.htm; accesses June 1, 2010.

7. Second Arab Oil Embargo, 1973-1974, U.S. Department of State online archives; accessed October 1, 2009.

8. Pew Research Center Publications, "Mapping the Global Muslim Population," Oct. 2009; http://pewresearch.org/pubs/1370/mapping-size-distribution-worlds-muslim-population; accessed June 1, 2010.

9. Patrick Johnstone, *Operation World* (Grand Rapids, MI: Zondervan Publishing House), 23.

10. Abdiyah Akbar Abdul-Haqq, *Sharing Your Faith With a Muslim,* (Minneapolis: Bethany House Publishers, 1980), Preface.

11. "Mapping the Global Muslim Population," Pew Research Center Publications, http://pewresearch.org/pubs/1370/mapping-size-distribution-worlds-muslim-population; accessed November 4, 2009.

12. Renwicck McLean, "Spain Considering Plan to Subsidize Mosques," *International Herald Tribune,* July 26, 2004.

13. John Vinocur, "Politicus: Where is the debate on Europe's Muslims," *International Herald Tribune,* November 9, 2004.

14. "France: Government Participates in Mosque Funding, in Islam in Europe," December 26, 2008; Islam in Europe (blog), Figaro.

15. BBC News; http://news.bbc.co.uk/go/pr/fr/-/1/hi/uk/ 72326 61.stm; February, 7, 2008; accessed June 1, 2010.

16. Samuel P. Huntington, *The Clash of Civilizations and the Remaking of World Order* (New York: Simon & Schuster, 1997), 256.

17. Such worldview differences include: honor killings (see http://www.gendercide.org/case_honour.html) and telling lies. "In (the west), telling the truth is 'right' and telling lies is 'wrong.' In the Middle East, people don't think of lies as being right or wrong. The question is, 'Is what is being said, honorable?'" Roland Muller, *Honor and Shame—Unlocking the Door,* (Xlibris, 2000), 51.

18. Among the evidences of Islamic advancement as a result of "new" wealth are:

   A. mosque construction in the West ("Eighty percent of the mosques built in the U.S. are built from Middle Eastern oil wealth." See http://www.rapidresponsereport.com/briefing-papers/ISLAM.pdf.)

   B. Construction of Islamic schools and universities and the expansion of Islamic education across Africa: "We can sum up the general features of the development and progress that Arabic teaching is experiencing in sub-Saharan Africa and that herald a bright future for the Arabic language in the following points:

+ The official introduction of the Arabic language in the curricula of formal education, at all its stages, in several countries of the region right after independence. This was the case in Chad, Guinea, Senegal, Mali, Niger and Nigeria.

+ The increase in the number of private community schools run by individuals and Islamic associations, and some Arabic and Islamic educational missions.

+ A sustained and notable increase in the number of Quranic schools and their spread in all parts of the continent.

+ The introduction of Arabic education in universities in many countries of the region.

(See http://www.isesco.org.ma/english/publications/Islamtoday/20/P6.php; accessed June 1, 2010.)

19. Recent public policy changes include:

A. "Muslim prayer rooms set aside for Muslim students in public high schools in US," *Chicago Sun Times*, November 29, 2001.

B. Halal meat served in public school cafeterias; Samuel Freedman, "For Fasting and Football"; http://www.nytimes.com/2005/10/26/education/26education.html; accessed June 1, 2010.

CHAPTER 3

1. *www.middle-ages.org.uk/the-crusades.htm; accessed June 1, 2010.*

2. Hugh Goddard, *A History of Christian-Muslim Relations*, (Chicago: New Amsterdam Books, 2000), 93-94.

3. Ibid., 95-96.

4. Ibid., 99.

5. Ruth A. Tucker, *From Jerusalem to Irian Jaya—A Biographical History of Christian Missions*, Grand Rapids, MI: Zondervan Publishing House, 1983), 53.

6. Ibid., 54; "...while in the forest alone with God, far removed from worldly distractions, he (Lull) meets a pilgrim who, on learning of Lull's chosen vocation, scolds him for his self-centeredness and challenges him to go out into the world and bring others the message of Christ."

7. Ibid., 55.

8. Samuel M. Zwemer, *Raymond Lull: First Missionary to the Moslems* (New York: Funk & Wagnalls, 1902), as cited by Ruth A. Tucker, *From Jerusalem to Irian Jaya*, (Grand Rapids, MI: Zondervan Publishing House, 1983), 57.

9. Hugh Goddard, *A History of Christian-Muslim Relations*, 120.

10. Ibid., 121.

11. Ibid.

12. The marks of this self-limiting theology of missions included: a) the conviction that the Great Commission of Matthew 28 was already fulfilled by the disciples, b) a view of the doctrine of election which made missions unnecessary, c) the understanding that the task of missions was given to civil rulers and not the Church, and d) a sense that the time was not ripe for missions because there were more urgent tasks at hand. Taken from L.L. Vander Werff, *Christian Missions to Muslims, The Record*, (Pasedena, CA: William Carey Library, 1977), 19, as cited by Hugh Goddard in *A History of Christian-Muslim Relations*, 122.

13. Ibid., 122.

14. The Student Volunteer Movement was an informing, motivating and recruiting phenomenon of the late 19th century in the U.S. and which traces its origins to a small student conference organized by Dwight L. Moody in 1886 in Mount Hermon, Massachusetts. As a result of this conference and what followed over the next 30 years, the SVM recruited and sent out nearly 9000 missionaries; http://www.christianitytoday.com/ch/bytopic/missionsworldchristianity/mobilizinggenerations.html; accessed June 1, 2010.

15. The Reformed Board, in refusing service to Zwemer and Cantine, was reflecting the prevalent attitude of the day that a mission to Muslims was not possible. *From Jerusalem to Irian Jaya*, 276.

16. The First Missionary Conference on behalf of the Mohammedan World was held in Cairo, Egypt, April 4-6, 1906.

17. *From Jerusalem to Irian Jaya*, 278.

18. Ibid., 279

19. The Joshua Project defines the term this way: A people group among which there is no indigenous community of believing Christians with adequate numbers and resources to evangelize this people group.

20. The Zwemer Institute of Muslim Studies is a 25-year-old program established in 1979 as the Zwemer Institute at the U.S. Center for World Missions in Pasadena, California.

21. John Bresnan, ed., "Between 1966 and 1976, almost 2 million ethnic Javanese, mostly from nominal Islamic backgrounds, converted to Christianity," *Indonesia: The Great Transition*, (New York and Oxford, Rowman & Littlefield Publishers, 2005), 107.

22. CBN report, "Muslims turn to Christ in Algeria," February 11, 2008.

23. "Millions of Muslims Converting to Christianity," *Salem Voice*, January 5, 2007.

24. Dudley J. Woodbury, "Why Muslims Follow Jesus," *Christianity Today*, October 2007, Vol. 51, Issue 10, page 81.

25. Ibid.

26. Ibid, 84.

27. Ibid.

28. Personal discussion with author, source to remain anonymous.

CHAPTER 5

1. The Holy Qur'an, Surah 53:1-15.

2. Jinn comprise a genus of beings somewhere between angels and men. Created, reportedly, of fire (Sura 55:14), like angels, they belong to the world of spirit. Like men, they are distinguished from angels in that their habitation is within the human domain, rather than in the heavens. Although theoretically neutral, most jinn are conceived as being bad. They are intensely jealous of human men, women, and children and as such, seek constantly for opportunities to injure them. Bill Musk, *The Unseen face of Islam: Sharing the Gospel with Ordinary Muslims* (Eastbourne: MARC, 1989), 38.

3. John Gilchrist, *A Comparative Study of the Proposed Revelation of the Qur'an* (Roodepoorte: Roodepoorte Mission Press, April 1989), 5.

4. Richard Bell, "Muhammad's Visions" *The Moslem World* 23:2 (April 1934), 149. Gabriel is traditionally identified by Muslims as the being seen by Muhammed in his visions and the messenger of the Qur'anic material even though there is no reference to him in this Surah. As Bell discusses in his article, it is not until Qur'anic passages written much later in Muhammad's life (during what is known as the Medinan period) that Gabriel is mentioned in this connection. In fact, the grammar and syntax of this passage suggest that Allah is the messenger whom Muhammad has seen. As a result of the development of Islamic theology between the Meccan and Medinan periods which, among other things more clearly codified the deism of Islam, one can easily see the reason for the substitution of Gabriel for Allah as the Qur'anic messenger.

5. John Gilchrist, *Muhammad and the Religion of Islam* (Roodepoorte: Roodepoorte Mission Press, 1986), 100.

6. Cyril Glasse, "Revelation," in *The Concise Encyclopedia of Islam* (New York: HarperCollins Publishers, 1991), 335.

7. As used throughout, the use of the term "supernatural" in reference to the source of dreams and visions is not intended to imply

only divine, as in heavenly, origin. It may also refer to demonic supernatural origin.

8. *The Concise Encyclopedia of Islam*, S.v."Koran," 231.

9. Bill Musk, "Dreams and the Ordinary Muslim," 164.

10. John C. Lamoreaux, *The Early Muslim Tradition of Dream Interpretation* (Albany, NY: State University of New York Press, 2002), 4

11. Ibid.

12. Ibid., 59.

13. *The Concise Encyclopedia of Islam*, S.v."Ru'ya," 339.

14. Ibid., S.v."tanzil," 397.

15. Ibid., S.v."al-Wahy," 416.

16. Bill Musk, *The Unseen Face of Islam* (Eastbourne: MARC, 1990), 186-187.

17. John L. Esposito, *Islam, The Straight Path* (New York: Oxford University Press, 1988), 90-95. Esposito lists and describes the Five Pillars of Islam under the headings, 1. The Profession of Faith (shahadah), 2. Prayer (salat), 3. Almsgiving (zakat), 4. The Fast of Ramadan (sawm), and 5. Pilgrimage (hajj).

18. Ibid., 198.

19. Ibid., 193.

20. Ibid., 214.

21. Esposito, Islam, *The Straight Path*, 110.

22. Musk, *The Unseen Face of Islam*, 230.

23. Ibid., 238.

24. *The Concise Encyclopedia of Islam*, S.v."Adat," 24.

25. *The Concise Encyclopedia of Islam*, S.v."Koran," 231.

26. It must be noted here, however, that it may not be fully possible to demonstrate the Gospel utilizing the appropriate means, symbols, and language of the Muslim worldview. The Muslim

worldview and biblical worldview are in conflict to the extent that at some level and with regard to certain affirmations (the identity and role of Jesus Christ), to embrace one is to deny the other. Nevertheless, accurate communication requires that the sender deliver the message in such a way and by such means that the receiver is able, without adapting to the sender, to understand the message to the extent intended by the sender. To do this, the sender must make use of forms, symbols, and language that adequately conveys the message—to the fullest extent possible—within the worldview of the receiver. So that after the message has been communicated, the receiver accurately perceives the message intended by the sender.

27. Roland Musk, *Honor and Shame: Unlocking the Door*, 33-34.

28. By "Western worldview" I mean to include those Western cultures that have been affected by Aristotelian epistemology which in brief, can be summarized by the conviction that truth (reality) can only be known through the five senses. As such, the supernatural world and interaction with it is considered unreal and impossible/irrelevant.

29. Musk, *The Unseen Face of Islam*, 230.

30. Ibid., 41.

31. Ibid., 91.

32. Hesselgrave, *Communicating Christ Cross-Culturally* (Grand Rapids: Zondervan Publishing House, 1991), 41.

33. Musk, *The Unseen Face of Islam*, 163.

34. "Western" refers approximately to late 20th-early 21st century post-modernism.

35. For example: The biblical worldview and the Muslim worldview both hold to the existence of God, of the importance and efficacy of prayer and the reality of the afterlife. The Muslim worldview and the Western worldview hold to the right of the superiority of some over others (i.e., men over women), etc.

36. For example: All three worldviews believe in right and wrong as a concept and all three promote the practice of public marriage and the privacy of the home, etc.

37. Morton Kelsey, *Dreams: A Way to Listen to God* (New York: August Press, 1978), 30.

38. Morton T. Kelsey, *The Other Side of Silence: A Guide to Christian Meditation* (New York: Paulist Press, 1976), 167.

39. Kelsey, *Dreams: A Way to Listen to God*, 22.

40. Ibid., 76.

41. Ibid.

42. Justo L. Gonzalez, *The Story of Christianity* (San Francisco: Harper & Row Publishers, 1984), 1:316.

43. Francis A. Schaeffer, *Escape From Reason* (Wheaton, IL: Crossway Books, 1993), Vol. 1, Book 2, *A Christian View of Philosophy and Culture*, 211.

44. Kelsey, *Dreams*, 18.

45. Ibid., 212.

46. Ibid., 228-229.

47. Ibid., 228.

48. Ibid., 233.

49. Ibid., 237-238.

50. Ibid., 240.

51. Ibid., 241.

52. Ibid., 7-8

53. Ibid., 24.

54. Ibid., 25.

55. Ibid., 26.

56. Sigmund Freud, *The Interpretation of Dreams*, trans. A.A. Brill (New York: The MacMillan Company, 1927), 492.

57. Ibid., 240.

58. Ibid., 494.

59. Ibid., 153.

60. Carl Gustav Jung, *Psychology and Religion* (New Haven, CT: Yale University Press, 1950), 102-6. In his study of dreams, Jung concluded that all dreams fit into the following categories: 1) Dreams of external stimulus; 2) Dreams of projected honor or dishonor; 3) Dreams of hidden personal conflict; 4) Dreams of hidden wishes; 5) Dreams of the future; 6) Dreams of warning.

Additionally, Jung categorized dreams into "personal" and "collective." The "personal" dream arises from the personal unconscious and relates to personal aspects of the dreamer's life. The "collective" dream, in contrast to the personal dream, often makes use of vivid images and symbols incomprehensible to the individual that are often understood only in terms of the historical and/or "mythological" significance of the images and symbols. Dreams of this nature have from antiquity been understood to communicate warnings and/or directives to the immediate or at-large community of the dreamer.

61. Ibid., 30

62. Ibid., 31.

63. Ibid., 38.

64. Ibid., 58.

65. Freida Fordham, *An Introduction to Jung's Psychology* (Baltimore, MD: Penguin Books, 1966), 102.

66. Jung, *Psychology and Religion*, 21-22.

67. Ibid., 73.

68. Ibid., 1-2. In the introductory comments in his book, Jung preempts his further discussion by describing his perception of his ability to competently address the implications of the philosophy and religion of the divine interaction of God and man. He notes, "Notwithstanding the fact that I have often been called a

philosopher, I am an empiricist and adhere to the phenomenological standpoint. I trust that it does not collide with the principles of scientific empiricism if one occasionally makes certain reflections which go beyond a mere accumulation and classification of experience. As a matter of fact I believe that an experience is not even possible without reflection, because 'experience' is a process of assimilation, without which there could be no understanding. As this statement indicates, I approach psychological matters from a scientific and not from a philosophic standpoint. In as much as religion has a very important psychological aspect, I am dealing with it from a purely empirical point of view, that is, I restrict myself to the observation of phenomena and I refrain from any application of metaphysical or philosophical considerations. I do not deny the validity of other considerations, but I cannot claim to be competent to apply them correctly."

CHAPTER 6

1. Five extraordinary accounts of Muslim conversion to Christianity via dreams and visions were documented and filmed in recent years by CBN and can be viewed on their Website at www. morethandreams.tv. DVD versions of these accounts in multiple languages (entitled, "More Than Dreams") can be ordered from the Website.

2. Constance Padwick was born in Sussex, England, in 1886. Active in the Student Volunteer Movement as a youth, a trip to Palestine in her early 20s changed the direction of her life forever. After several years working in the home office of the Church Mission Society, she eventually moved to Egypt where she began an overseas missionary career that spanned nearly four decades and took her to Palestine, Sudan, and Turkey. Padwick's major contribution to the world of missions was in her writing. In addition to editing a significant mission journal of her day, she wrote a wide variety of materials for Muslims, biographies of significant missionaries, and tracts and articles designed to inform and awaken the church to its responsibility to reach Muslims with

the gospel. This excerpt of the writings of Constance Padwick is taken from a 1939 reprint in the International Review of Missions, of a work she published under the title, *The Master of the Impossible*, 50 years after her departure to Algeria.

3. Isabella Lilias Trotter (1853-1928) was an artist and missionary for over 38 years to the Muslims of Algeria. After serving God in England for a time with the YWCA, she went with her own funding to Algeria to serve God there. In 1888 she founded the Algiers Mission Band which merged with the North Africa Mission in 1964 (later Arab World Ministries). Lilias Trotter wrote and illustrated several books including; Parables of the Cross, Parables of the Christ Life, and a book for Sufi Muslims, The Way of the Sevenfold Secret. Her devotional writings which were first published in a periodical and later as a booklet entitled, "Focussed", inspired Helen Lemmel to write the now famous hymn, The Heavenly Vision (Turn Your Eyes Upon Jesus). Taken from A Passion for the Impossible: The Life of Lilias Trotter, Miriam Huffman Rockness, Harold Shaw Publishers, Wheaton, Il, 1999.

4. Ibid., 207.

5. Ibid., 208.

6. Ibid., 208-209.

7. Ibid., 209-210.

8. Patricia St. John, *Until the Day Breaks, The Life and Work of Lilias Trotter* (Loughborough, England: OM Publishing, 1990), 36.

9. Ibid., 211.

10. Ibid., 210-211.

11. Ibid., 212.

12. Ibid., 213.

13. Ibid., 214.

14. Ibid., 215.

15. Ibid.

16. *Through a Glass Darkly: Knowledge of the Self in Dreams in Ibn Khaldun's Muqaddima, in The Muslim World*, Vol. LXXV, (Hartford: The Duncan Black MacDonald Center, 1985), 36.

CHAPTER 7

1. According to Webster's Online Dictionary, a *worldview* "consists of a more-or-less systematized set of opinions on the structure of the universe, the meaning of life and one's relationship with society." A person's worldview helps them answer the questions of life such as, "what is important," "how does this work," "what does this mean," and "what do I believe." Everyone has a worldview (which is for the most part inherited from family and prevailing culture) though for most people it resides in the background of their thoughts, beliefs, and actions.

   A *biblical worldview* would be the collective patterns, structures and resultant beliefs and practices that are based upon the teachings of the Bible and which include such things as a divinely directed creation of all that is, the reality of a moral law which applies to all humankind, the existence of God, angels, demons, and Satan, and the eternal destiny of individuals—some by virtue of saving faith, in the presence of God, others, by virtue of moral rebellion, in a state of eternal suffering.

2. Freida Fordham, *An Introduction to Jung's Psychology* (Baltimore, MD: Penguin Books, 1966), 102.

3. Ibid., 32.

4. Ibid., 35.

5. Ibid., 45. Interestingly, C.E. Padwick, whose article is cited later, relates some findings of a missionary woman (Lilias Trotter) in Algeria during the 1800's. In her diary she notes that the dream and vision accounts that were used of God for spiritual benefit in the lives of Muslims were nevertheless colored by the subjects prevailing cultural situation. So, Algerians always dreamed of

Christ dressed in white that either reflected the biblical depiction of Him that was propagated by missionaries at that time, or the fact that Arab men all dress in white unless Europeanized. Additionally, a Central Asian Muslim during a pilgrimage to Mecca, dreamed of Christ dressed in green robes, the Muslim sacred color.

6. Ibid., 46.

7. Boyce Bennett, *An Anatomy of Revelation* (Harrisburg, PA: Morehouse Publishing, 1990), 98.

8. Ibid., 92.

9. The presence of angels in Jesus' life begins with angelic visitations to Mary (Luke 1:26-38) and Joseph (Matt. 1:20-24), the shepherds (Luke 2:9-13), continues with an angelic visit at the end of his 40 days in the wilderness (Matt. 4:11); shows up frequently in his teaching (Matt. 13:39, 41; Mark 12:25; Luke 12:8,9; John 1:51) and ends at the tomb, after his resurrection (John 20:12).

10. The closed biblical canon refers to the 66 books of the Old and New Testament Scriptures, referred to collectively as the "Holy Bible." The canon of Scripture was effectively closed—that is to say, no new writings could be added, and nothing included could be removed—by the affirmation of the early church councils: Carthage (A.D. 397).

11. By this time in the Book of Daniel, Darius has become king of the Medo-Persian Empire, displacing the Babylonian monarchy.

12. See Matthew 1:20; 2:12-13,19.

13. See Luke 1:11,26.

14. An auditive event is a type of vision in which a voice is heard, but no one is seen speaking.

15. The Book of Revelation, notwithstanding. In Revelation, however, the visionary experience of the apostle John is explicitly given to transmitting the content of the book to the apostle for the purpose of writing it down, as opposed to providing personal instruction, warning, or encouragement.

16. The Pharisees and Sadducees of Paul's day differed in their respective beliefs with regard to the spiritual world and the afterlife. The Pharisees held to the existence of angels, demons, and the afterlife. The Sadducees denied them all.

17. The ensuing discussion has significant implications relative to the role of dreams and visions in conversion. If in fact Saul received sufficient salvific content from the dream alone to repent and turn to Christ, Ananias' role is that of a post-conversion encourager and assimilator into the Church. If Saul's Damascus Road encounter was in and of itself not salvific, then Ananias' role (and by implication, the Church) is that of facilitator into personal faith.

18. Hans Conzelmann, *Acts of the Apostles* (Philadelphia: Fortress Press, 1963), 71.

19. The apparent contradiction to this chronology that Paul appears to refer to in Galatians 1:11-12 can be understood as follows: Paul's reference to his reception of the gospel through a revelation of Jesus Christ refers to his vocational call to ministry, which occurred sometime after his conversion (probably during his 14-year stay in Arabia). His reference to the arrival of the gospel in his life from Acts 22 refers to his conversion subsequent to his Damascus road encounter as a result of the help of Ananias.

20. Morton Kelsey, *God, Dreams and Revelation* (Minneapolis, MN: Augsburg Press, 1991), 86.

CHAPTER 9

1. See Romans 10:14 NLT.

2. Quranic reference to Jews and Christians; the Book being the Bible.

3. http://www.theologywebsite.com/history/crusades.shtml; accessed December 17, 2009.

4. Jacques Ellul, *The Subversion of Christianity* (Grand Rapids, MI: Wm B. Eerdman's Publishing, 1986), 97.

5. Ibid., 99.

6. Ibid., 100.

7. Ibid., 101.

8. Ibid., 112.

9. http://www.jihadwatch.org/2008/09/al-qaeda-declares-coptic-priest-zakaria-botros-one-of-the-most-wanted-infidels-in-the-world.html; accessed December 17, 2009.

10. Rick Love, "Discipling All Muslim Peoples in the 21st Century," *International Journal of Frontier Missions*, Vol. 17:4, Winter 2000.

11. For a brief introduction to the current growth of the Church in Algeria and to some extent, Morocco and Tiunisia, see the following youtube video: http://www.youtube.com/watch?v=mL5nJpXeCSo&feature=related.

12. *Daniel Ammann*, "The Real Reasons why the Swiss Voted to Ban Minarets," *The Huffinigton Post*, December 1, 2009.

13. http://www.break.com/usercontent/2008/3/Fitna-The-Movie-Geert-Wilders-documentary-about-Islam-478140.html, accessed June 16, 2010

14. Ian Traynor, "'I don't hate Muslims, I hate Islam,' says Holland's Rising Political Star" in *The Observer*, Sunday, February 17, 2008.

15. http://www.maldiveisle.com/history.htm, accessed June 16, 2010.

16. http://news.bbc.co.uk/2/hi/south_asia/3930765.stm; accessed December 21, 2009.

17. John Piper, *The Roots of Endurance, Invincible Perseverance in the Lives of John Newton, Charles Simeon, and William Wilberforce* (Wheaton, IL: Crossway Books, 2002), 18.

18. Ibid., 19.

19. See Romans 8:18-25.

20. See Second Corinthians 6:2-10.

21. See Romans 5:3-5.

Contact the Author

Rick Kronk would appreciate communicating with you by e-mail concerning any questions that you may have as a result of reading *Dreams and Visions*. Perhaps you've experienced a dream or a vision that you would like to share with him. He can be contacted via e-mail at:

rick.kronk@yahoo.com

Additional copies of this book and other book titles
from DESTINY IMAGE™ EUROPE
are available at your local bookstore.

We are adding new titles every month!

To view our complete catalog online, visit us at:

www.eurodestinyimage.com

Send a request for a catalog to:

Via Acquacorrente, 6
65123 - Pescara - ITALY
Tel. +39 085 4716623 - Fax: +39 085 9431270

"Changing the world, one book at a time."

Are you an author?
Do you have a "today" God-given message?

CONTACT US

We will be happy to review your manuscript
for the possibility of publication:

publisher@eurodestinyimage.com
http://www.eurodestinyimage.com/pages/AuthorsAppForm.htm